IMPACT

Where Passion and Purpose Makes a Difference

ISBN 978-0-9883438-3-2

Printed in the United States of America
Instantpublisher.com

Printed in the United States of America Amazon.com

Acknowledgements

I wish to personally thank all the collaborative contributing Authors for their transparent writings, knowledge and other help in creating this book.
You all ROCK!!! THANK YOU!!!

Table of Contents

Impact

We hope it's ok if we start with asking you a few questions. We really want to help engage you in creating a difference and in making an impact in your life. Are you living the life of your dreams? Are you doing what you've have dreamed of doing? Have you ever asked yourself, what is my purpose or why I am here or why am I doing this or why is this happening to me? Have you ever wondered why some succeed in this game called life while others barely get by? Are you making an impact on your life, your finances, your happiness or even your business? Are you making an impact on others' lives, others' finances, the happiness of others or even others' businesses? We were all born for a purpose, with a purpose. Sometime during life, many choose to "give up" on their dreams. So many decide to stop pursuing what that purpose is or could be, and they start existing instead of living to make an impact.

The word *impact* means to have a strong effect on someone or something. The terminology "make an impact" is such a dynamic phrase within itself. How limited or limitless we see ourselves determines the magnitude of impact we believe we can or cannot make. We believe that everyone can make an impact in life and in the world, no matter how big or small. It doesn't matter if we touch one life or millions. We each have the opportunity to make a difference. Sometimes, circumstances and/or events can make an impact on a person or people. Local, regional, national and world events can have an impact on people either positively or negatively.

How have situations and circumstances impacted how you show up? Have they ignited the fire in your belly so you have been driven to pursue you passions, create your dreams and create the impact you were born to make, or have these circumstances created doubt, taking the wind out of your sails?

We have found that through our journey of working with thousands of entrepreneurs, there is an underlying reoccurring theme. They want "more": more money, more clients, more business, more time, more fun, more happiness, just more. More is such a relative word. The word *more* is a comparative, so the first question we ask them is, more compared to what? What we have found is that people can easily tell us what they don't want, yet they struggle in telling us what they do want, and when they do manage to share what they do want, it is so ambiguous that it becomes unachievable.

As you will see by the collection of authors in this book, each of them is out to make a massive impact by pursing their passion and fulfilling their purpose. We have the pleasure of knowing each of these dynamic entrepreneurs personally, and there is one very common denominator with them all: they are all living their passion and purpose and making a difference in the lives of the people they touch and serve. While they are making a difference in so many different areas of life and business, the ripple effect is making a massive impact. Our wish is that their stories touch you, inspire you and motivate you to pursue your passion, create your purpose and make the impact you were born to make.

No matter where you've been, what choices you have made and where life has taken you, every day is the first day of the rest of your life, which means every day is a new beginning. Every breath we take and every second we have allow us to be the being we were born to be, to make the impact we were chosen to make. No matter how small or big, or how insignificant or significant we think who we are or what we do is, everything said, done and experienced makes a difference. Think about the butterfly effect.

"LinkedIn to Possibility" – From *I Do to Undo to Redo*
By Rhonda Sher

We all have a story deep inside us. Some are too scared to reveal their inner journey; others fear being looked upon as a failure, and some do not know how to put their story into words.

I am a daughter, wife, mother, and woman who has been in the corporate world. I am an entrepreneur who has written three books, given hundreds of talks, and has a black belt in shopping. In addition to having "ADD," I also have "ALD," addictive learning disorder. Ever since I can remember, I've been on a never-ending quest for knowledge, inspiration, hope, and light.

For me, life is a smorgasbord of amazing, wonderful things to learn, people to meet, places to go, and something or someone new to find or experience. It has not been a life without challenges or ups and downs, but it has been a fun ride. I hope my story will inspire you to reach into your soul and to discover your bliss in the midst of chaos.

My name is Rhonda Sher, and this is my story.

Today, I am married to the man I had my first date with at age 19.

That night, I told my dad, "Yeah, this is the guy I'm going to marry." He laughed at me, and said, "Kid, you've got no idea what you're talking about." But little did he know, six years later, he would be walking me down the aisle to meet the man of my dreams, the man I knew I would love forever from the moment I first laid eyes on him.

Looking back, 24 seems young. I guess, when someone knows, they just know, and in that moment, it seemed so right. I was ready to begin my life with my first crush, my first love, my first everything. You can imagine the excitement and expectation of all the perfection to come.

From Boston to California, we lived 28 incredible years together and have two wonderful, beautiful daughters as the result of our love. Now, 26 and 28 years old, I'm proud of who they are, who they're becoming, and the thread they are weaving into those around them.

As they say, "life happens." Often, it happens in the most spontaneous and unexpected ways. As much as we try to plan for everything and anything, there are some things we'll never truly be prepared for.

After 28 years of marriage, we hit a wall. We came to a halt. We were stuck. Ultimately, it led to our divorce. In what seemed like a blink of an eye, our love went from bliss to divorce.

It didn't happen overnight. The time leading up to the actual split was a blur lived by a person I could no longer recognize: me. Where was I headed? What was this dark path ahead of me? It was beyond petrifying. I couldn't find the light. I couldn't find my way out of the black vast forest, where I felt completely and utterly lost. It seemed like it had been years.

So many suffer and feel alone through tragedy and disappointment. I was overwhelmed. My mother was dying. My career as a speaker was hanging by a thread. I was facing a scare so many face: cancer. The dream house we owned was upside down to the tune of $400,000. Add to everything, menopause had taken over my body as if I was possessed. Like an emotional landmine, I had no control of my emotions. My "personal summer" would flash over me like a heat wave at the most inconvenient times. I yelled at my kids and husband. I over-committed to many things, overpromising and under-delivering. I could not stop the Niagara Falls of tears that I woke up and went to bed with every day. My life was spiraling out of control in ways that led me to lose control of nearly everything in my life: my marriage, my kids, my business, and most of all, myself. That was my life in 2009. Does that sound familiar?

I think one of the most petrifying moments one can face during their life is the fear of losing themselves. It was as if I could no longer recognize the person I was. What's worse is my family didn't recognize me either.

I don't blame anyone for what happened: my husband for wanting the confident, loving woman he married, who was now absent; my kids, who wanted the mother they used to know, who was rational and there for them and not a hormonal tornado.

I knew I needed help healing, and I had to find the strength, courage, and light within me. My spark was buried deep, and I needed to reignite the flame that had flickered out over the years.

In 2009, I was alone, lost, and without a self-sustaining income. My world came crashing down, and I was lost within the cracks of oblivion. It was as if I was watching a television show of someone else's life.

Fortunately, I received spousal support from my ex-husband. I never thought I would have an ex-husband; it simply was a thought that had never entered my consciousness. I knew several things: I had my health, regardless of the divorce. I still had my family and friends, and I was resourceful. I had the spark of hope that everyone possesses inside their soul. Knowing that gave me enough light to move forward in the darkness, amidst the chaos and destruction, to find the life I wanted to live as fully as I had.

I'm not writing this to gain empathy or for self-pity, self-doubt, and self-defeat. I'm writing this to acknowledge that we, as people, don't always need to have everything figured out. We don't always need to have it together. We don't always have to be the best versions of ourselves every minute of every day.

I'm writing this in acceptance of my past, in appreciation for my present, and in hope for my future, because it's not about who you are when you fall in defeat; it's who you become when you stand on your own two feet and rise higher than ever before. This message is for the hopeless to get back up again. It's for everyone to see it only takes one spark to light a fire and create a connection.

Being a single woman in my fifties was not the way I thought my life would turn out. I had not been on my own since college, and I had truly never lived and experienced life alone. I went from dorm life to an apartment with roommates to getting married in my twenties and leaving everything behind to move across the country with my husband.

My childhood was not one that equipped me to know how to be a great wife or mother or how to handle hard times. I can now see it was a gift that gave me the strength I needed to find the resources to handle the tough times. I just did not know it at the time.

Following the events of 2009 and my divorce, I found comfort from strangers who became my friends, guiding me through therapy and coaching. Every day, I'm reminded how grateful I am for the people, places and experiences that inspired my journey out of the dark, beaten path, consistently encouraging me and helping me see there is light at the end of the tunnel—I had what it took to reach within and find my way out.

The reality was, I had to find a way to support myself when I chose to no longer receive the spousal support my ex-husband so generously gave me. I was not living lavishly, but I knew I had to earn enough money to continue living the same lifestyle. Some things, like hair and nails, are not negotiable (said with a smile). My options were to deplete my savings or hit the bricks and start selling.

The choice was simple: I started selling by sharing the gift of living benefits life insurance.

I was not going to give up my "retail therapy"—I still had a black belt in shopping. I was not going to be a Walmart greeter if I depleted my savings, so I got into high gear and did what I knew how to do: connect, serve, and make things happen. But wait, there's more!

I started using LinkedIn as the primary vehicle for finding clients and networking. I knew LinkedIn very well. After all, I had written a book on it and had spoken to hundreds on how to use it. Time to practice what I preached. I discovered that, while I was successful in selling life insurance, using, teaching, and sharing LinkedIn and networking was my passion.

During that time, I also developed another relationship and was engaged. I discovered, however, it wasn't going to be the relationship of a lifetime. In 2015, I ended the relationship and went full-time into my passion: LinkedIn and being a speaker and connector. I was free, successful, and hopeful about the future.

Then, the real miracle happened when the stars aligned. Bob, my ex-husband, and I, through the magic of a course called Wisdom (how fitting) and Landmark Education, found each other again! This was never going to happen, yet through the paths of growth, change, and transformation that each of us took after our split, it allowed us to see each other again as if for the first time. I never would have imagined, at the end of the tunnel where the light hit my face, I would look up and see my husband. It was as if I ended up right where I started, only this time, I had found myself and broke through the chains that had kept my heart and mind hostage for so long.

I call Bob my "wasband" and husband. He truly is and always will be the love of my life. I consider myself blessed, fortunate, and thankful every day to have had a second chance at life, love and happiness with him and for the realizations we had when we were apart.

Life is truly unrecognizable, and being remarried to him, I don't believe I have ever been this happy, this in love, this free, not only with him but, most importantly, with myself.

I found the work I love: helping professionals find clients using LinkedIn. What an oxymoron, because doing something you love is never work; it's your passion, it's your career, it's the light of your life and the spark of inspiration that keeps you going

I still experience addictive learning disorder and am now studying NLP and going to seminars and continuously working with coaches. My goal is to help my husband retire from the corporate world in two years and to start a consulting practice. Nothing would make me happier than to contribute to his dream of being free from the corporate world. Those who know me will tell you I don't stop until I make my dreams a reality, so, with confidence, I can say I'm well on my way.

I have often been asked how I became a LinkedIn expert, a speaker, trainer and co-creator of an online course that teaches people how to hire sales professionals using science. The answer is, I kept doing new things until I found what fit. I knew that, no matter what, I would come out on the other side where there was light, love, and the resources I needed. You will too.

During the time between my divorce and remarriage to Bob, there were many struggles, obstacles and surprises. One of the most defining moments was on a date with the dean of a local college. It was more like an interview than a date. He asked me what my greatest strength and greatest weakness was. I told him my strength was being a resource and connector, which has helped in every aspect of my life. I told him my weakness was that, if he asked me what was on the table at the restaurant where we were sitting, I could not tell him. I could tell him everything that was missing. He told me that a graduate student could tell what was missing and an undergraduate could tell what was on the table. That was a lightbulb moment for me. What I had perceived as a weakness all my life was truly one of my greatest strengths. It was a blind spot that now glowed brightly.

Looking back on my life, I wouldn't change anything. The pitfalls, the mistakes, the pains, and wrong turns—I wouldn't change any of it. It all led me to this moment, and from where I'm standing, the view that lies ahead is breathtaking.

But, if I could talk to who I was when I was young, I would tell her…

1. Spend time with your family and friends and the people you love. There will always be time for work. Be someone who gives and is a stand for others. Remember, life is about serving.

2. Pick your battles. I would have told my younger self not to argue with my kids or act like a kid—be the mom who loves them unconditionally, listens to them, supports their dreams, and knows that, sometimes, they just won't like you and that is ok. I would tell my younger self, be fully present wherever you are, be a person of integrity.

3. Be there for your husband in every way, to let him know how important he is and how happy he makes you. Learn his love language and speak it. Have his back and be a stand for him and for yourself.

4. Be brave and trust your intuition to do what you love in your career. Take chances. Know it is ok to try different things until you find what fits. Be ok with the fact that the road often contains potholes and detours. The only thing you can control is how you react to what happens, not what happens. Be committed to what you want, not attached, or you may miss something extraordinary.

5. Remember to breathe and that 98% of what you worry about never happens. Trust that there is a

power bigger than you that will lead you exactly where you are supposed to be. Listen to the little voice. It usually is telling you something you need to hear.

The impact I want to have on the world is to know I have made a positive difference in the lives of others. I want to know I shared my gifts freely, I made someone's day brighter, and every life I touched is a little better than it was before I was there.

My journey is just beginning. I spend most of my time doing "done for you" LinkedIn profiles and speaking about leveraging LinkedIn. I am also creating online courses on LinkedIn, business networking, face reading, and taking the guesswork out of hiring. I love helping people create a digital footprint on LinkedIn to attract clients and referrals, while showing up as they really are: powerful, strong, and ready to be of service to those who need them.

I hope my story has touched you in some way or given you hope if you are in a dark place or shined a light even brighter if you are where you belong. Know that everyone who comes into your life is there for a reason or a season; they are all our teachers and there are no accidents, only gifts that sometimes come in the most unusual packages.

I am grateful for all the gifts in my life, my most precious ones being Stefanie, Vanessa, and Bob. You are my light, my loves, and my teachers. I love you.

Rhonda Sher is a nationally recognized expert in business networking and LinkedIn. She is the author of *The Two-Minute Networker*, *The ABC's of LinkedIn, Get LinkedIn or Get Left Out* and *How to Avoid the Business Card Pile-Up: 52 Ways to Boost Your Business with Business Cards.*

Rhonda is the expert at teaching CEOs, small business owners and entrepreneurs how to leverage LinkedIn and convert relationships to revenue. Rhonda's natural humor, interactive approach and 20 years of business experience has brought her into the forefront as a sought-after national keynote speaker and trainer. She teaches powerful, practical techniques and insider secrets to take your profile to profit using LinkedIn. Rhonda is a wife, mother and an entrepreneur on steroids whose mission in life is to make a difference in the life of every person she touches. She can be reached at yourconnectionconsultant.com, 760-515-2822, Rhonda@yourconnectionconsultant.com

"Even though everyone tried to stop me…. I was… AM
Unstoppable"
by Maureen Pisani

I was a happy, rambunctious little girl until I was 8½ years old. That unforgettable Easter Sunday, in Malta, when I was startled awake with my dad moaning, "Wake up Maureen, I'm dying," was the end of my childhood. My quick thinking and actions literally saved my dad's life. He had had three massive heart attacks in one week…and survived. During the next 60 days, while he was in a medical coma, at home, I came to a decision. I would become a doctor to find ways to stop these awful heart attacks from happening. However, a short while after that, I realized I despised needles, so at the wise old age of 9, I amended my decision. I publicly declared, from that point, I was going to "help people without needles."

True to my word, I did. Initially, I was an X-ray technician in a 1500-bed hospital, the only one on the island. I thrived in helping my patients get the best service and treatment I could offer.

Once I immigrated to the States, I worked as a medical historian, again "helping people without needles." I got hurt. I incurred severe bilateral cubital tunnel syndrome. It was horrible. My three bosses, all orthopedic surgeons, recommended surgery. After 10 surgeries, 5 on each elbow, I was still in horrendous pain. Each surgery was followed by weeks in a cast and months of physical therapy to attempt to bring the elbows back to normal. Nothing worked. I was taking 24 pills a day, 14 of which were pain medications. I lost 80% grip strength in my right hand and 75% in my left hand. It was awful. The doctors, having run out of options, came up with a solution. They declared me 100% disabled, placed me on Social Security, offered me a lifetime supply

of medications, and washed their hands of me! And…I was 30. Do you think I came to this country to be on Social Security at 30?
Absolutely NOT!

The more desperate the situation became, the more I begged God to give me a life…and boy did He answer my prayers!

Out of the blue, I stumbled on hypnosis. I had no clue what it was. Thankfully, it was scientific, and I took to it like a duck to water. I was in my element. Only…I couldn't write notes, and I was a note-taker. So, I was referred to a hypnotherapist, who nonchalantly approached my disaster as if it were nothing out of the norm. I was skeptical, suspicious, a non-believer if you will. However, after the first session, the pain from the shoulders to the wrists disappeared! I was curious. I simply had to find out what he had done. I went in for my second appointment. Again, he asked me questions, I responded, and again, he hypnotized me and the next morning…NO PAIN! All that horrendous continuous pain GONE! It didn't come back, and it won't.
This mess had taken 6 years, 10 surgeries, and over 25,000 tablets! And, in two sessions…done! History! Gone!

I simply had to understand how that happened, and it has been the exploration of a lifetime. Once I graduated from that college with Top Honors, I continued advancing. I became the only hypnotherapist in California to have been an instructor and director in two nationally accredited colleges. I co-authored a neuroscience paper through UCLA, authored 8 hypnotherapy books, and produced 25 CDs.

Immersing myself in the hypnotherapy world has allowed me to remove all limitations. Most people live life from the "if only" perspective while I take the chance. I know what being stopped feels like, and I hate it. So, I go on. I keep going. I look into the worst-case scenario, and yes, I am cautious, but I keep going. I've been able to achieve things I never thought I could.

It's really a remarkable system to utilize. The only way I find out if I can do/create X is by giving it a shot. What's the worst that can happen? If I find out I'm not able to do X, oh well…at least I experienced it. So, I've always gone for that "unreachable" achievement, because what if I did reach it? How much better would my life be? And, that's what keeps pushing me forwards. I always want to find out what's around the bend. It's interesting, because my curiosity has opened an incredible number of doors that, if I had been hesitant, would have remained shut.

When I see kids around 8/9/10 years of age, they all look incredibly young. At those ages, I never felt like a little girl. I just felt like me. I took myself seriously. The easiest way to describe my childhood is chaotic, and regardless of my chronological age, I had to do what I had to do to ensure we were all safe and everyone stayed alive. Disaster would not happen on my watch.

So, as I think of and look at little Maureen in my mind's eye, I would share with her how courageous she was. Maureen always did what she knew was necessary, but she wasn't told whether she did a good job. Nobody, not once, ever told her she had stepped up to the plate when she saved her daddy. I would compliment her on her ability to jump into action. She knew Daddy was seriously sick, and if something happened, he could die. Even at that age, Maureen knew what death was. A lot of great aunts and uncles had died, and she knew death was permanent, yet she handled it all.

I would also tell Maureen she was beautiful. Her grandma once took her aside and told Maureen her sister was the beauty of the family and she better study. That advice helped her advance academically, but she needed to be told she was beautiful, smart, energetic, talented, and unstoppable. I would also tell her she was smart, and that is a fantastic trait to have. I would encourage her to shine as brightly as she could. She was defiant in a good way. She knew she had strength, talent, and persistence, and she utilized those characteristics to help others, family primarily, and others around her. Herself…rarely.

Today, having become more self-aware a few years ago, I am ready to share my strengths with others on a larger platform. Now that I'm an established hypnotherapist, an NLP trainer, a master in therapeutic guided imagery, and a Master III in Reiki, I can help, in many ways, and I do.
Here are some results….
One of my mentees' parents had a massive brain tumor that required two surgeries to be excised. She was in her 70s, and the procedures were daunting and life-threatening. We worked electronically and prepared her for surgery. Both surgeries went tremendously well. Instead of what was expected—walking with a walker in maybe six months—using hypnotic suggestions resulted in her climbing stairs with a cane in three weeks.

A young lady feared the dentist and needed all four wisdom teeth to be extracted. The dentist estimated an hour per wisdom tooth, due to the young lady's intense fears. After preparing her hypnotically the day before, all four wisdom teeth were extracted in 45 minutes. Both the dentist and the young lady were surprised with how she reacted to the procedure.

As a brand-new, soon-to-be mommy, a lady had heard the horror stories of how many days she was expected to be in labor while giving birth to her first born. After working with me, she was surprised to experience that it only took 47 minutes from her first contraction to holding her daughter.

After experiencing intense lower back pain for over a year, a lady requested additional diagnostics, only to discover she had been walking on a broken hip for over 14 months. We worked together online. We specifically prepared for the surgery. Hypnotic suggestions were given so the body knew how to react during surgery and to guide her through her recovery regarding the healing process, range of motion, and regaining strength and endurance. Specific recordings were done for pain management. She regained full range of motion, with full strength, and a normal gait in 50% of the time other patients took. Throughout the entire ordeal, the heaviest medication she took was Tylenol.

An adolescent came into my world because of an embarrassing condition. As a tween, she still wet her bed. She was limited on what she could do or where she could go because of this big secret. After working with her and retraining the unconscious mind of what to do, she attended the desired camping trip with all her girlfriends and was completely successful and free!

In a case of mistaken identity, a young man, while walking out of a bar, minding his own business, was brutally attacked by several thugs. He was beaten to a pulp and suffered multiple fractures including facial fractures. He had experienced level 8 pain for decades. The facial pain was excruciating. He had gotten 12 Botox injections to his face every month, only to have the level of the pain decrease to level 6. In the first session with me, utilizing several hypnotic techniques, his pain had reduced to level 2.

A young lady, who had an incredibly close-knit family, was going through a very stressful period in life. She experienced severe psoriasis. From the collarbone down, her entire body was covered in huge dollar-sized blisters. It was so aggressive and so irritated that people would actually stop her in the store to ask if she was contagious. We worked together for three sessions, where I gave her three recordings that she listened to for three months. At the end of the three months, she was blemish free, she was calm, and she was back to being her beautiful self!

A young man came to me with a very specific request. He wanted me to help him stop chewing one particular knuckle. As a child in first grade, he chewed his fingernails, and the teacher made fun of him. Then, not to chew his fingernails, he chewed on a pencil. Then, the teacher made fun of his black teeth (from the lead in the pencil.). So, he started chewing on his knuckle. He had done this for over 40 years. We worked together, and after two sessions, the knuckle chewing stopped. Now, years later, his knuckles are still smooth.

A family man entered my world because he needed to stop smoking. He had smoked since his teenage years, and at the time, he was smoking 3 ½ packs a day. It was something he knew he had to stop but didn't know how. During our 3-hour session, between the cognitive NLP exercises and the hypnotic suggestions, he unconsciously became a permanent ex-smoker. It's been 7 years since that appointment, and he is still a permanent ex-smoker.

An incredible lady came to me with the worst loss of her life. Her child had passed away. It was horrendous. She was in so much pain she couldn't find a reason she should stay alive. Through our collaboration and hypnotic suggestions, we got her unconscious mind to ease the pain, offer her peace and tranquility, and start a small spark of hope. These were enough to start an unconscious foundation, so she could live day by day and participate in her and her other children's lives.

A lady came to me heartbroken, betrayed, and furious. Her soon-to-be ex-husband had done all the unthinkables. And to add insult to injury, she had to face him in court. We worked together not only to have her calm down in the courtroom, but to have her be calm and appreciative with herself. She maintained her composure in the court proceedings. She was professional and polite when responding to him. She showed her best side. After the process was done, she was free, with her dignity and integrity intact.

A young lady showed up in my world wanting more. As a high introvert, she had been a spectator in her own life, hardly participating in the events she had wished to experience. She wanted more. More of everything. However, she didn't have the slightest idea how to go about it. The biggest emotion she connected with had been fear. Working together, I introduced her unconscious mind to various aspects of life, introducing the initial concepts, the experiences, and the safety involved in these experiences. Over a few months, this young lady evolved into a beautiful woman, who is now thriving in her fully experiential life and loving it!

My primary mission is to share the benefits of these alternative modalities with the public to teach how easy it is to implement these modalities to create and receive undeniable results. I've stated to thousands that when "my mind and your mind collaborate, we can move mountains!" and I truly believe it. I've run two practices in San Diego and Los Angeles, had a crazy life, drove 400 miles a week, and when my friends asked me why I worked that much, my answer was, "Because I can help two sets of clients instead of just one!"

I thrive in teaching effective techniques to others, so they can have a "better today, every day." My plan is to reach millions and effectively teach them how to upgrade their lives in a positive, comprehensive way.

Maureen Pisani C. Ht, T. NLP., founder of Pro-Thrive Science-Based Hypnotherapy, is also a motivational speaker and author. She has been in practice for over 12 years. She's the only hypnotherapist in California to have been a director and instructor in two nationally accredited colleges. Maureen co-authored a paper through the Neuroscience Dept. at UCLA. She is the resident therapist at the Chopra Center at La Costa, in San Diego, California.

In an effort to offer the best service and results to her clients, Maureen continues her studies extensively. She is an NLP trainer, a master in guided imagery and a master in

Reiki energy work. Maureen has authored 8 books and produced 25 CDs.

Maureen specializes in SIDE-EFFECT FREE pain management, be it physical, emotional, financial or career pain. She helps clients, on an individual basis or in group settings, to overcome chronic situations that hinder their progress.

Maureen focuses on helping individuals have a better today, every day. She is always looking at how to serve and how to implement her "it only gets better" philosophy!

Feel free to contact her at: www.prothrivesbh.com OR https://facebook.com/prothrivesciencebasedhypnotherapy or 619-252-2253.

Always Beginning a New Journey
By Jennifer Ervin

I am….
I used to be scared to complete that sentence. It was always
negative or possibly modest. I know my "I am" is different
from the "GREAT I AM." Throughout the different paths
I've taken on my journey, also referred to as "my dash,"
I've learned to see the impact I have on one person, which
leads to hundreds. How? If I impact one person through my
work, my friendship, my companionship, my conversation,
anything really, then I impact the people they impact.
Maybe not directly, but I know the impact is there.
I am…a performer!
When I was younger, I wanted to be an actress. I couldn't
imagine doing anything else. I'm sure my parents, though
supportive, kept hoping I would change my mind and pick
a career with more stability. It didn't happen the way they
wanted. I attended a 4-year university and got my
bachelor's degree in theatre arts with an emphasis on
acting. Done. "Now my career in acting can begin. I know
everything there is to know about the acting world." Yeah,
if only it were that easy!
After I graduated, I appeared in many stage shows. I would
audition for commercials and television. I would even
audition and appear in student films. Yet, I felt
unfulfilled…as though there was more out there in the
world for me to be a part of than driving to and from
auditions and rehearsals. My main joy came from doing
shows with my improvisational troupe, The Greenstone
Players, around Orange County and Los Angeles County.
Through this group, I learned so much more: business,
leadership, teamwork. We were together over 10 years.
I am…a massage therapist!
As my husband and I were going on our sixth year of
marriage, I decided it was time for a family. I was yearning

for parenthood. All I wanted was to be a mom, and at any cost. I had been working at a construction office as an admin. I decided this j.o.b. wasn't going to help my acting career. I also did not want to leave my baby with a daycare or babysitter. I needed a job that would allow me to work around my baby's needs. Within three days of attending a spa day for one of my girlfriends' bridal showers, I was attracted to the idea of being a massage therapist. I loved the idea of the flexibility to go to auditions, and I had this grand illusion that I could massage with a baby tied to my back like a papoose. I would soon find out those ideas were fiction-based.

I attended massage therapy school and fell deeply in love with it. I loved learning everything I could about the human body and about the different massage modalities available. I saw how incredible the body is and what was possible when working on the body. It was more than just relaxing the muscles. It was truly life changing. Deep healing—both in the body and in the mind—could occur, bringing the body and mind into perfect stasis. With this newfound passion, I quit my job at the construction company and became a therapist at the Four Seasons Hotel and Spa. Within a year, I was massaging in a rented room, in a day spa, and in my home, and at the Four Seasons.

I am…a strong mom!

It was a glorious day in January that I found out our first attempt at fertility was successful. I was pregnant, according to the stick. I was in disbelief but so excited to have a lifelong dream come true. Everything was moving along smoothly with the pregnancy until 4 ½ months in. I was working at the Four Seasons, when I felt a rush of pain through my lower and mid-back. I immediately thought I was losing the baby. The sheer panic I felt of that thought intensified the pain in my back and in my heart. I was rushed to the hospital, where I was admitted and made my temporary home for the next 10 days. After five days in ICU, having blood transfusions and even a visit from the chaplain (it was that serious), I learned I had a tumor wrapped around my kidney that had ruptured and was causing me to have severe internal bleeding. The doctor assured me everything was okay with the baby, but I had to spend the remainder of my pregnancy on bed rest. It was a trying time. I couldn't work. I couldn't go out. I had to be catered to, which was a challenge for me, since I had always been so independent and was used to catering to everyone else (I am a massage therapist, so nurturing and caring for everyone else is second nature to me). But the thought of dying and not giving my baby a chance to be born well and healthy terrified me, and it was enough to make me endure this challenging situation. Kyra was born a healthy, vibrant baby, and five months later, I had "Frumor the Tumor" (a name I gave to my tumor to remind me I could instill humor in my life, despite the seriousness of my condition) surgically removed. The surgery required cutting into about 10 muscles and a separation of the ribs. Recovering from a surgery of this magnitude, while taking care of a five-month-old baby, was not an easy task. Yet, being able to hold my precious baby in my arms reminded me of how fragile life can be and how resilient and strong human beings are.

I am…a teacher!

As a new mommy, and after massively invasive surgery, I was unable to do much of anything, especially a physically demanding job such as massage therapy. I remained at home, nurturing my daughter and myself back to health. I then received a call to teach at the massage school where I had been a student. I was nervous about this leap, mainly since I was insecure about teaching such in-depth information about the human body, but it was an exciting opportunity that would allow me to make some income and teach a subject I was passionate about. It would be gentle enough that I could continue my recovery from the surgery with ease. I said YES, and I'm so glad I did! I was filled with a sense of purpose as I facilitated the beginning step for students who wanted to start a new career in such a loving field as massage therapy. I found that, by teaching in the classroom and then teaching in the lab, I could keep myself immersed in the field while recovering. After several years of teaching, I was finally able to massage again. I kept my teaching position at the school, but I started taking massage jobs for clients once again. I was back in the game.

I am...an entrepreneur!
When my husband and I got engaged, we decided, when we had children, I would remain at home with them. That's why being a massage therapist was so appealing. There was flexibility in that kind of profession. I would be able to massage clients out of my home or after my husband came home. After 2008, times became tough for everyone in the country. Massage became less of a necessity and more of a luxury for most people. Kyra was 3, and I had my newborn, Kylie, to raise and only my husband's income to sustain us. He was working tirelessly. He worked 2 jobs full-time. Many days, he would just sleep in his car, so he could go from one job to the next. Finally, after my little one started kindergarten, we agreed I would begin working more than just the occasional classes I was teaching at the massage school. That's when I was inspired to begin a chair massage business. It didn't really take off because I was busy working as an independent contractor for other massage businesses and didn't have the time to invest in marketing. However, in 2015, I decided to give it another go with the chair business. In 2016, I realized I wanted a regular mobile massage business to be my source of income. Thus, I began Healing Touch Mobile Massage in January. By February, I learned how important networking

was. I joined a referral network group and felt my business take off from referrals. This is where and when I received a flyer to attend a Success Boot Camp led by Stacey O'Byrne. I had no idea what to expect. In fact, I expected this presentation to be completely about the referral group I had joined. Little did I know my life was about to be changed forever and completely for the better.
I am…awake!
She shared information I had never heard before, and something in me became curious about how these learnings could help me expand my business. I didn't know, at the time, it wasn't just my business that was going to expand. My life would never be the same. What I learned in those eight hours as I sat in the Success Bootcamp was enough for me to choose to take the courses offered by Stacey and Pivot Point Advantage. It was something called NLP (neuro linguistic programming) and integrated time line therapy. I signed up for the first set of courses, and upon completing them, I was ready to move forward with the next set. I could see my life changing daily, and I wanted to see what else was possible for me and my business.
"What am I taking this class for? What does this have to do with massage? Why am I here? This learning is too cerebral for me as a massage therapist! I think I need to quit!" That was me during a panic attack I had in class one morning. I could feel the blood drain from my face. I was ready to get up and walk out. But God said to me, "Calm down. It will all make sense soon enough. Just stay right here." I obeyed. I didn't get up and run out to my car like I wanted to. Instead, I let the course continue to wash over me.
That night, at 2 a.m., when I was in a deep sleep, I was suddenly awakened. I grabbed my phone off the nightstand and began typing. I was out of it. I was still asleep, mentally. That's how I know God had given me a big piece of my puzzle as to why I was in this class. This is what appeared in my Notes on my iPhone: Breakthroughs and

Bodywork: A Facilitated Journey to Healing Your Body, Inside and Out.

"What? What does that mean?" Before I could conjure up an answer, I fell back to sleep. At the next class, I told this revelation to Stacey, who just smiled and said it was awesome. I think she knew this revelation would have greater meaning, and more pieces of the puzzle would fall into place.

I am now awake. I'm listening like never before. I'm seeing like never before. I'm talking like never before. I was reborn with eyes wide open. Colors look different. People seem different. Who I am today, after these classes, is someone who knows and honors who she is. I am more confident. I have more courage to take calculated risks. My relationships are more authentic. My business is flourishing, and the impact I'm making in people's lives is profound and transformational.

I am…a Breakthroughs and Bodywork therapist!

As I began my journey with my new tools in the toolbox, I realized there is a need in the world to have bodywork and mindset shifts at the same time to be effective. I created, through obedience, the Breakthroughs and Bodywork technique, incorporating mental and emotional breakthroughs for people, then two days later, they will get it released from the body. You see, cells carry our emotions and our trauma, and they settle into muscles. I have my clients consciously release them from the muscles through my bodywork. It's been amazing to see the long-term effects of this technique on my clients. Chronic issues are no longer chronic. Unexplained pain in areas is gone. People see through their obstacles, and their bodies are sustaining them to get things done. Whether people want to feel freedom from stagnation in their relationships, career, money situation, or any other major conflict in their lives, Breakthroughs and Bodywork truly does have a profound IMPACT on their lives.

Jennifer was born and raised in Southern California. Her childhood dream to be an actress was pursued until her mid-30ss. She got her degree in theatre arts and performed in many theatres around Los Angeles. Then she found a new love: massage therapy. She has worked as a licensed massage practitioner since 2003. In the meantime, she became a mom to 2 beautiful daughters who are her world. She became a leader in her community and learned quickly how to improve her skills in that arena. She has been working on her professional and personal development for the past several years and believes that the birth of her technique would not have been possible if not for her new learnings. She continues to learn and improve on her life, which she owes all to God. She is looking forward to the momentum she will pick up from doing and not just dreaming.

Decisions (Actions), Force and Me
By Andrea Gewirtz

I don't remember when I started to dream about it.

At first, it felt rather perplexing that Newton's law of motion was anywhere in my consciousness. It had been so long since I had studied physics. And yet, at least twice a week, I would dream about F=MA.

What did it mean?

Explicitly stated, it is force equals mass times acceleration. It expresses the relationship that the speed at which an object moves (force, or velocity) is equal to the weight of the object (mass) multiplied by the speed at which the object is moving. Okay, you've heard it all before in high school...so what? Dreams and dreams about...this? I'd wake in the morning feeling strange because the dream had been so vivid. It was always the same: the equation materializing in front of me, interspersed with images of my own life.

On and on it would go some nights...searching, sifting and sorting. Each morning, I'd consciously state to myself, "What has this got to do with my life?" The rote, sarcastic reply was: "Something. Or you wouldn't spend so much time unconsciously flashing through the Rolodex of your life regularly looking for it."

Sure, it was Newton's law of motion, but I felt a strong personal connection with it. I had the sense that the equation was present in my daily life—that it was everywhere. This left me with questions. What is force? What does it look and sound like? And the mass? Am I the mass?

And then, a dream was answered with another dream.

In some ways, it was more like a memory or a recollection. The answering dream recalled one of the greatest challenges of my life. In one night's rest, I relived a terrifying diagnosis and the months that followed.

It was the summer of 2001. I was on assignment in St. Louis, Missouri, as the TD of Talk of the Nation, and we were setting up for the live broadcast of a Town Hall meeting. I had just run the Marine Corps Marathon in the fall of 2000, and I thought I was invincible. Then, out of nowhere, I could hear my own heartbeat. Loud. Fast. Pounding. A day into the weeklong assignment, I started to feel pretty lousy. I went to Urgent Care in St. Louis to get help.

They told me I was dehydrated and that's why my pulse was a little elevated. It seemed reasonable, so I went back to work, running at 100 miles per hour while getting the live show ready. What was not as reasonable was the rapid weight loss I experienced in the week while I was on location. After 6 days on the road, I came home 11 pounds lighter.

My internist didn't take my concern too seriously as I explained the loudness of my heartbeat and how I was suddenly breathless and couldn't run anymore to prep for the next Marine Corps Marathon. I had been running 5 miles a day to stay fit for the upcoming race, and now I was breathless while just standing still. My heart sounded like a freight train trying to burst out of my body. On the outside, I looked fine, but I knew that all was not well within. The uncertainty shook me to my core. I didn't know what it was. I was scared.

I sought out a cardiologist. There were sideways glances and raised eyebrows when I entered the waiting room. I was young and looked healthy. It seemed strange for me to be there, but the nurse immediately understood why I was freaked out when he took my pulse. "It's the Dance of the Bumblebees," he joked. To this day, I am grateful for his cheerful demeanor as it quickly put me at ease. The bigger blessing was the cardiologist who immediately suspected an overactive thyroid as he allayed my worries. I was not going to have a heart attack! Blood tests revealed a hyperactive thyroid, and I was promptly sent to an endocrinologist.

As nice as he was, the endocrinologist assumed that I would be okay with immediate radiation to treat my thyroid and that I would resign myself to a lifetime of taking a synthetic thyroid hormone replacement. Nope, not so fast. With the cause identified, fear gave way to curiosity. I wanted to understand the turn of events in my body, so I went into high-research mode to learn all there was to learn about this mysterious gland known as the thyroid.

My research made me rather resistant to solutions like radiation, removal or a lifetime of synthetic thyroid medications. I had come to learn that this gland had a lot of control over the entire organism known as "me." The delicate balance that keeps our bodies running smoothly was thrown into disarray when my thyroid went into overdrive. The thyroid gland, pituitary gland, and the hypothalamus must work together synergistically in order to regulate your bodily functioning of everything from your brain to your liver. I wasn't ready to part with her as she held court with an impressive cadre of my personal command center operatives. I expressed my concerns with the endocrinologist and asked for more holistic alternatives. He could not recommend one: "I am not aware of any that really work." The lack of options only galvanized me to find them myself.

I asked him for a deadline. I bargained with my doctor to let me figure out a treatment methodology that was more in alignment with my beliefs. I'd have to face surgery and the hormone replacement if I couldn't find a way to regulate my thyroid within the next 4 months.

I reached out to my friends involved in holistic medicine. I had weekly acupuncture treatments and biweekly osteopathic treatments to balance my body. I got more rest. I diligently adhered to a new diet. I changed my behaviors for sleeping and self-care, recalibrating my body into a healthier state. There were a lot of incentives, too. I wanted to be able to get pregnant. I wanted to be able to run again. I wanted my hair to stop falling out and I wanted to get a good night's sleep.

Together, with the care of an acupuncturist, a naturopath, and an osteopath, my thyroid hormones were brought within a normal range. I was astonished and elated, and I had done it in 4 months! Even my endocrinologist was amazed that I had accomplished what I set out to do.

When I awoke from this dream that was also a memory, I was awash with emotions: fear, elation, devastation, triumph and gratitude that my thyroid continued to function normally.

Overcoming hyperthyroidism naturally was a pivotal point in my life, and in more ways than one. Was it easy? No. There was so much to learn and to test that it was often bewildering. I didn't always know what I was doing. All I knew was that I wanted to return to good health and that I would do everything in my power to get there. I didn't know how to put the pieces together, but I found kind and knowledgeable people who did.

Not only did I radically change my lifestyle, but I realized I had the ability to radically change my life. In reclaiming my health, I unmasked my strength and my energy, to be a force.

Then it hit me.
Just by existing, we have a certain force (F). We are mass (M) in acceleration (A).

Multiply us humans by our actions, and we generate force. Our actions may impact the world in ways great or small, but even our smallest choices set life itself into motion.

(F)orce = Me (Mass) x Action (Acceleration)

A woman (M) faced with a frightening diagnosis decides to seek out alternative treatments (A). She takes actions to change her daily habits, and the impact (F) is immense: she heals.

A gymnast (M) defies gravity to nail a dozen consecutive back handsprings (A). Mass multiplied by action, with the effect (F) of taking our breath away.

First responders (M) make it their sole purpose (A) to save someone in a crisis (F).

A teacher's (M) effort (A) to move every mind in a classroom—regardless of their varying propensities—helps every child to understand a previously unknown fundamental (F).

(M) is a constant; it's who we are. (A) is trickier to fit into this metaphorical equation.

How come?

Action is an accelerant prompted by the decision to act, to be in motion.

According to Newton's laws of motion, the greater the acceleration, the greater the force.

As my health crisis unraveled and I was tasked to find answers, my activity, my drive, and my purpose were single-mindedly fixed on recovering my health. I took massive action to make massive changes to myself. The analogy of Newton's physical laws of motion couldn't be more apt to describe my momentum and my drive.

Activity, regardless of the magnitude/size, is an accelerant. As I learned one new strategy to help myself, it was immediately employed to test and determine if it could move me closer to "normal" test result ranges. Every action moved me from my starting point (illness) and towards the destination (improved health).

So, is (A) purpose or action? As far as humans go, I think they go hand-in-hand and they feed each other to move us all ever forward. And, like Newton's laws of motion, consecutive, focused actions generate more velocity (momentum) and have a corresponding greater impact on your life.

That's what we are: mass in action.

And when we decide to act, we ignite ourselves to be massive in our impact.

Andrea is the CEO of her dynamic multi-faceted and eclectic life. Like many creatives, she balances motherhood and "solopreneurship" with ingenuity and grace. Originally trained as an operatic singer and an electrical engineer, her first professional years were spent as a technical director and engineer for National Public Radio in Washington, DC. Desiring an even fuller life, she married and had two children. Professional opportunities sent her and her family out West to California. In California, a child with unique learning skills created a need for Andrea to find an outlet that would be professionally rewarding and economically beneficial. Through an interesting course of events, Andrea discovered the world of sales and networking. Today, she is a passionate creator of teams of men and women who desire to have a positive work life balance all while enriching their respective communities and the lives they touch.

The Vacation That Rocked My World:
How One Small Misstep Gave Me a Huge Break
By Deborah Reed-Anderson

When I met John, the beloved man who would become my second husband, he declared his core purpose was to craft a life of integrity and normalcy. The majority of our mutual attraction was rooted in that same, seemingly mundane desire. As a child of divorce, however, my tumultuous home life rocked with instability and dysfunction. Heading into adulthood, I vowed to find balance and integrity by building a life that mattered. In my search for stability and distinction, I stumbled upon accounting, while attending a local community college near home in Southern California. To me, debits and credits infused sense into my imbalanced, nonsensical world. Because I liked that company books must balance and be clean to earn respect, I declared accounting was the profession for me. After three years of study, I landed my first bookkeeping job in private industry, working for a small software development company.

After a glorious, five-year honeymoon at work, my cherished employer was acquired by a large corporation, and I was eventually laid off. Wandering from job to job over the next fifteen years, I gained accounting experience in multiple industries, including utility software development, educational products, and environmental engineering. Despite my lack of an accounting bachelor's degree, compensated for with several years of night school and a churning desire to excel, my numerous employers approved of my hard work. Ultimately, I earned promotions and increased responsibilities during my many employment tenures. The issues I faced at each opportunity, however, were boredom and isolation. No matter where I decided to play bean-counter, I eventually felt insufficiently challenged in my duties and experienced minimal interaction with coworkers. Although each organization initially exuded promises of excitement and purpose, the routineness of the accounting cycle, with four stark walls and a computer, followed me to every position.

After twenty years in private industry, my decision to migrate to public accounting was sudden and somewhat reckless, since the idea of long tax-season hours never appealed to me; however, my longings for change and meaningful work, with the prospects of using my skills to help businesses within the community and increasing interaction with others, trumped my preference to maintain a 40-hour workweek. When a large, well-respected accounting firm hired me as a bookkeeper to work with their small business clients, I believed the quality of my work life was about to improve one-thousand-fold.

The greatest of hopes, when based on desperation, provide the greatest pain when the walls of aspiration crumble. With 120 firm employees, including 16 partners, I soon learned my whimsical demeanor, bright red hair, and penchant for donning cloche hats to accentuate my wardrobe charmed the minority of my traditional-minded colleagues, despite my solid professional qualifications and unwavering work ethic; as a result, I quickly became relegated to the organization's 1% nerd population. Because of my status as an outcast, opportunities for challenging and interesting assignments diminished, and invitations to lunch, after-work happy hour engagements, and weekend gatherings from my coworkers gradually ceased. Adding to the angst was my increasingly unhappy home life: my husband, unemployed for many years, grew increasingly bitter over his jobless state and emotionally vacated our marriage. As the years passed and the frustrations mounted, I realized I was cheating myself out of a fulfilling life by choosing to remain in miserable circumstances. My path towards change began with the difficult decision to split with my husband after twenty-five years of marriage. As my financial situation grew increasingly fragile, I clung to my job at the accounting firm, despite the constant despair I endured going to work. Nearly two years after I split with my first husband, I met John, and we realized a few weeks into our courtship that our respective searches for an eternal partner had ended. A couple of years later, joyfully, we wed. Although life became happier, my job distress continually loomed over me.

Since one of the many interests John and I share is travel, we decided to take a road trip in July 2013. We chose Austin, Texas, as our ultimate destination, since we were craving an authentic barbeque meal (we both adore eating, too). After loading our truck, we began the three-day trek to the Lone Star State, arriving at our hotel late on a Wednesday evening. We felt overcome by exhaustion from days of driving, sightseeing, and barbeque-binging. As John reclined on the bed in our room, the power surged, causing a brief electrical outage. When we discovered the phone service was also disrupted, I decided to walk downstairs and notify the hotel reception clerk. Since the stairs were right outside our fourth-floor room, I decided to use the opportunity to get a little exercise and work off some of my calorie-laden lunch. In a few short moments, however, my life would change forever.

As I began walking down the steps of the hotel, I missed a step and found myself airborne, launching head-first toward a wide concrete pillar. Instinctively, I shielded the top of my head with my left arm and my face with the right. With both knees bent, and wearing only flip-flops on my feet, I slammed onto the landing and heard a loud, nauseating crunch. The right flip-flop propelled over my head, and with both legs tucked under my body, waves of pain shot from my feet, through my legs, and to my pelvis with burning, symphonic force. I felt sick.

After uttering various, profanity-laced variants of "Ouch!,"
the first coherent thought that entered my mind was,
"Looks like I won't be returning to work on Monday.
Yay!" Despite the intense physical pain, I felt immediate
alarm over the indirect joy I felt as a result of this mishap.
The troubling feelings were temporarily suspended during
my visit to the local hospital emergency room, where
technicians x-rayed and examined my feet and ankles,
swollen to the size of two beefy cantaloupes. When the
head nurse informed me of the x-ray results, I was shocked:
two broken ankles and a broken right foot. After securing
my damaged bones and ligaments in matching splints and
gifting me a wheelchair, the hospital staff wished John and
me safe travels as we began our three-day journey back to
Southern California.

Once John and I arrived home, I visited an orthopedic
surgeon, who assessed my injuries. Although I would not
require surgery, both feet would need orthotic boot fittings;
furthermore, I would be wheelchair bound for at least six
weeks and would require the use of a walker for several
subsequent months. Although the news numbed me, I felt
relief that my injuries would heal, commingled with
confusion over the directional shift my life took in a matter
of days.

During the first two weeks of my disability, while brooding
in front of the family room television in my wheelchair,
with my orthotic boots and bottle of Vicodin as my
constant companions, I fretted continually about the
inevitable return to my job at the firm. At the beginning of
the third week, my worrying evolved into severe anxiety,
and I began to cry one afternoon during an episode of *I
Love Lucy*, which, in hindsight, is pretty grim. As I rolled
into the bathroom to retrieve some tissues, I stared into the
mirror at an appalling image: a crimson-cheeked, pucker-
eyed, snotty-nosed, fifty-year-old female face that seeped
of self-pity. It was ugly. Very ugly.

A couple of hours after my blubbering bender, since I still felt uncompelled to deal rationally with my panic, I performed the only act I could think of at that moment: I relied on my faith and prayed. The next morning, lying in bed after the most restful night's sleep in days, I sensed an internal voice speaking softly to the depth of my core: "You are not returning to that job." The anxious chatter that had been shouting discouragement at me for weeks immediately ceased, and exuberance replaced agitation. Although I had no plan to transition to a new professional path, one thing was cerebrally understood: Rather than hunt for another dissatisfying job, I would seek a fulfilling and purposeful existence. In a matter of minutes, after my inner revelation, I wheeled clumsily to my laptop to research my authentic destiny that I intrinsically realized: entrepreneurship. Forming my own bookkeeping consulting company. Me? Really? Yes. Unequivocally. Wow.

My third week of disability ended with positivity instead of despair, and I surfed the web with confidence, pouring over articles that offered guidance for aspiring business owners. The weeks swirled by as I immersed myself in studies of marketing strategies for bookkeeping entrepreneurs by participating in webinars and reading blogs and books by industry thought-leaders. Because of my physical limitations, John assisted by acting as chauffeur, taking me on short outings to open a business checking account and rent a mailbox at the local mailing center. Two months after the accident, I ditched the wheelchair and was using a walker. My foot and ankles, along with my spirit, steadily strengthened.

During the final few weeks of my disability period, I performed many pre-opening tasks for my home-based business, such as designing my business cards and creating a simple website. Since the doctor allowed me to remove the orthotic boots for increasingly longer periods, I began driving again. Because my networking circle was nonexistent, I joined a weekly networking group, whose members graciously admitted me, even though my business was not yet operational, and soon, I began making business contacts. I was amazed how many kind people I began meeting as I pursued this new segment of my life. I was ecstatic and felt accepted and valued. A few days later, I drove to my accounting firm to inform my boss of my intention to resign my bookkeeping position after my release from disability. To my surprise, he offered his sincere congratulations and support of my new endeavor. When I left his office and the firm for the last time, I felt validated and like I was on the right life path.

In December 2013, my orthopedic doctor officially released me from disability, and Balance with Integrity, my bookkeeping company, began operations immediately thereafter. Although I started my practice with zero clients, I refused to allow discouragement to ooze into my brain. Besides my weekly networking meetings, I began attending every local business event I could find. Walking into crowded conference rooms, shaking multiple hands, and sharing my passion with total strangers about my quality bookkeeping consulting services became easier and—shockingly—extremely enjoyable. In several weeks, opportunities began trickling in: I conducted a bookkeeping training session for the staff of a networking colleague; a webmaster I had met at a networking breakfast inquired about my services and eventually became my first regular client; and a client from my old firm, after discovering on social media that I had started my own practice, called and transferred her company's bookkeeping engagement to Balance with Integrity.

For many years, I believed working in the bookkeeping profession was a major source of my unhappiness. Boredom and feelings of isolation caused me to flee private industry after twenty years; however, my nine-year experience in public accounting, while offering a variety of learning experiences and opportunities to help people who feared or hated maintaining company accounting records, drained all satisfaction and joy due to my constant struggle for respect and acceptance from many firm colleagues and managers. Thirty years of my life passed before I realized that what I was doing for a living was never the issue: the problem was how I chose to do it. Birthing my own bookkeeping practice four years ago resulted in my attainment of peace and balance, while serving clients with integrity. Happily married to John and savoring entrepreneurship, I feel oddly grateful for that little misstep in Austin, Texas, in July 2013. Sometimes, your biggest break presents itself in the most unexpected way.

For over thirty years, Deborah has enjoyed a career in the accounting and bookkeeping profession. Prior to her leap into entrepreneurship, she spent twenty years employed in private industry before performing a nine-year stint at a large accounting firm. In 2013, Deborah founded Balance with Integrity, LLC, a bookkeeping solutions and QuickBooks® training and consulting services company.

Every company's financial records tell a story. Deborah thrives on assisting business owners and managers with producing accurate financial reporting and equipping business professionals with the ability to interpret the underlying themes of their companies' financial reports. Deborah appreciates good storytelling and values the art of exceptional communication with clients, as well as with people in her personal and professional circles. She earned her bachelor's and master's degrees in English literature in 2007 and 2011, respectively, from California State University, Long Beach. Deborah resides in Southern California with her husband John, spaniel canine sons Riley and Gorgeous, and bunnies Princess Penelope and Beatrice, who are the genuine queens of the household.

My Voice- My Power
By Laine Proctor

When I first set about answering the question, who am I, I marveled at how differently I would answer this question today than even six months ago, much less two and a half years ago, before I started on my present path of evolution. Of course, looking more deeply, I see I am and have always been deeply dedicated to a path of truth seeking and truth telling. Not in the sense that a journalist or a scientist does; I am not particularly interested in revealing major truths of humanity to masses or people, uncovering our communal secrets in a breathtaking "ah-ha" moment. My seeking has always been on a more personal level. If I had to boil it down to one question that I have sought to answer over and over again, it is "Why do I hurt and how can I make it better?"

I could produce many reasons for this: my parents' divorce, the fact that I was a sickly child and struggled with my weight from a young age, my mother's apparent desire to hide everything that went on in our home (including the fact that she was a Cuban immigrant) from the outside world. And at times, I have looked to all these causes and conditions. I hurt because... – and the answer that I inevitably sought on the other side of that knowledge was that knowing would somehow decrease the pain.

It didn't work.

Neither did becoming a rabid overachiever, being voted "Most Likely to Succeed" by my graduating class, or getting a full academic scholarship to one of the nation's most prestigious universities.

Neither did booze or drugs or losing weight or refusing to lose weight or hanging out with what I thought were the coolest people.

Neither did romantic relationships. Or lack of romantic relationships. Or casual sex.

One thing works and has always worked.
I remember the first song I ever learned. I was three years old, and one of mom's best friends—an exuberant ex-nun named Joanie after whom I had named my favorite doll— was giving me a bath. Being that I am the second of five girls, my mom often had help from a revolving cast of characters to juggle the infants and toddlers during those years. As I demanded for the 20th time that Joanie make more bubbles for me to play with, she used a diversional tactic, shrewdly saving the rest of the baby shampoo, and asked if I wanted to learn a song.

    I have a little turtle. His name is Tiny Tim.
    I put him in the bathtub to see if he could swim.
    He drank up all the water. He ate up all the soap,
    And now he's sick in bed with bubbles in his throat.
    Gurgle gurgle gurgle…glug!

I must have sung that song 1000 times. In the bath, at bedtime, in the morning, during meals…. Tiny Tim was pretty much my constant companion, until his post was eventually usurped by Little Orphan Annie telling me the sun would come out tomorrow, Sandra Dee singing about summer lovin', and a host of musical angels.
Without realizing it, I had discovered my direct connection to all the unadulterated joy this glorious universe of ours has to offer. All I had to do was open my mouth and sing. And it is all I wanted to do.

I was passionate about sharing my dream and my talent with everyone. Not everyone was as passionate about hearing it. In fact, it seemed that, almost immediately, I was presented with a host of reasons to become discouraged.

One: I was fat. Fat people don't get to be famous singers. Two: the way to become successful was to get good grades and go to college, not pursue some pipe dream. Three: no one seemed interested in helping me to get the training and support I needed. I lived in a small town far, far away from the Hollywood dreams that I wanted to get my hands on, and everyone there seemed to have, in my opinion, equally small concerns. My mom and dad were engrossed in the business of providing for five kids, and it was often clear that it was a stressful and outburst-inducing business.

I interpreted this as a lack of love for me and a general lack of concern for the things that were important to me. Not only did they not want to give me dance lessons, but they didn't want to hear me sing the same song for the eight-hundredth time. I just didn't understand it. I made up my mind fairly early that I would be getting out of my family and out of Bakersfield as soon as I could.

So, I set about doing things I thought would get me there. I remember, in third grade, I won my class spelling bee. It was the first time I remember getting any positive attention in school. I had struggled with anxiety, social awkwardness, and being away from home since pre-school. But when I won that spelling bee, it flipped a switch in me. I wanted to do well and get as many accolades as I could. I also wanted to be a cheerleader, but I was not chosen. My family indicated, in not so many words, this was due to my weight issue. I threw myself that much harder into academics. And clubs. And theater. And student body. Basically, I was doing anything that would keep me out of my house, look good on my college resume, and make me more visible to faculty and fellow students. I didn't think about why or how—I just said yes to all of it.

Meanwhile, my parents' marriage had imploded, and I experienced a stream of confusing and heartbreaking domestic situations. I felt absolutely torn between my parents, like it was impossible to love them both without betraying someone. I also felt like I had to look out for my three younger sisters, as my oldest sister had gone away to college. During this time, I was also sexually abused by a friend of the family. I dealt with all this by telling myself I would be gone soon enough. "My life is ahead of me, and soon, none of this will matter," I would tell myself. And by drinking. Drinking made me feel like I could have fun and be one of the crowd. I told myself it was OK as long as it didn't interfere with my grades.

I was cheered on by the fact that my accomplishments were stacking up, and my "plan"—build insane momentum by working like a freight train and hope it gets me somewhere—seemed to be working out. I was accepted to Stanford University. Apparently, no one from my high school had ever done that on academic merits. It was so momentous an occasion that they put the news in my high school's morning announcements. However, I opted for UC Berkeley upon their offer of a full scholarship. I also wanted to be near San Francisco, as Janis Joplin was fast becoming one of my musical idols.

I took off for Berkeley with the idea that life was beginning. And it was. It was beginning to get even more confusing. My balancing act of academic success became even more challenging with access to limitless booze, drugs, raves, and gay bars, as I was beginning to explore my sexuality.

The process of doing what was expected of me to win approval became infinitely more complex as I was exposed to so many different influences. Also, the obvious next steps were not so obvious anymore. By the time I graduated, I had been advised that I should pursue a career in academia. I had lived abroad and had started an honors thesis with one of the most respected art historical minds of the day. I had performed in front of hundreds of people, taught poetry in prison, and written my first songs. I had also gone to therapy, suffered major depression, quit my honors program, and graduated feeling pretty aimless, but with the same dream I started with. I still just wanted to sing.

And I am still guided by that force today. Today, I see my talent for and attraction to music as a gift that I was given freely, and I do everything I can to give that gift back. I am so grateful that, through the many trials I have had with addiction and toxic relationships and self-doubt, I have always had a way to turn inward and connect with that limitless source of joy and peace.

I am grateful that having that experience has always given me hope that more is possible.

A little over two years ago, I was newly sober and coming out of a destructive relationship of six years when I found Pivot Point Advantage. I had met Stacy O'Byrne in my professional networking group and, whereas I had been skeptical, I was at a place where I could see the possibility in what she had to offer. I took a giant leap of faith.

In the course of a year and a half, I completed all her Success Mastery Academy courses. Whereas, I had previously found that motivational and empowerment trainings left me feeling motivated for a short time, only to inevitably fade into an expensive and ineffective memory, this was very different. I found myself changing almost without realizing it. Part of this I owe to Stacy's level of mastery over her subject matter and her integrity as a teacher, coach, and human being. The rest I believe I owe to myself and my willingness to show up and to give the absolute best of myself, this time for myself.

Over the course of these two years, I have tripled my income through my bookkeeping firm, recorded an album, fallen in love with someone who is incredibly kind to me and good for me, helped other women to get and stay sober, mended my familial relationships and, at 43, become pregnant with my first child.

Most importantly, and preceding all these things, I learned to appreciate the woman I am and everything that has brought me to this point. I learned in Success Mastery Academy that there is no failure, only feedback. When I am not getting the results I want, it's my responsibility to examine that feedback and do things differently.

Whereas, I started my bookkeeping business as an opportunity to scrape by on my own schedule and not have to answer to a boss, I now see it as an opportunity to help as many creative individuals and entrepreneurs as I can to fulfill their dreams. Whereas, I saw my musical talent as the failed dream of someone rapidly ageing out of the industry, I now see it as a beautiful gift that has had time to develop and am seizing the opportunity to make the best music I have ever made. Whereas, I accepted whatever came my way in relationships, I now give fully of myself and ask the same from my partner. Whereas, I expected my family to be who I needed them to be, I now love, accept, and even enjoy them for who they are. Whereas, I never allowed myself to admit that I wanted to be a mother, I now know I am the woman I am meant to be. I know I am strong, kind, resilient and nurturing, and everything I have ever experienced has made me so, and I will do a beautiful job of raising this child.

Looking back at my younger self today, I have so much compassion. If I could, I would tell her that, in the end, the only approval that matters comes from within. I would tell her to keep singing her song always.

Laine Proctor, owner of Proctor Financial, is an experienced bookkeeping professional and QuickBooks expert. She harnesses the power of the robust network of QuickBooks products and expertise to do everything from analyze and re-educate current users on how to improve their efficiency, to setting up systems from the ground up for new and first-time business owners.

She loves empowering business owners to focus on the things they love about their business while handling the paperwork headaches. She finds it gratifying to help others achieve their creative and financial goals.

Comparative Living
By Derlene Reeves Hirtz

"Theo is in the 95th percentile for height compared to the other babies." So says the doctor who measures my grandson on his medical checkups during the first year of his life. I could not agree with the doctor more: My grandson is way above average! I laugh to myself as I think, "No kidding, you should get to know his parents; they are way above average too!"

It appears as if, almost immediately upon birth, our life centers around being compared to someone else. First, as children reach milestones of height and weight, then rolling over, walking, and talking. Once they begin school, they are immediately compared to other children, academically. As a former teacher, I get the necessity of it. I really do. My point: comparative living happens upon birth and lasts throughout our life.

Eventually, what happened for me is that I began comparing myself with everything and everybody:

"I am not nearly as pretty as Cindy."

"John can eat anything and not gain weight. He is lucky, and I am not."

"Why is it people work a lot less and make so much more money than me?"

"Chris is so smart; I could never compete with her."

"The Jacksons have a bigger house than us. We should really sell and buy a bigger one."

Any of this sound familiar? Why do we do that? Compare ourselves to another person's standards? The "why" for comparative living is not important, but the recognition that we are doing it is vitally important.

Somewhere along my journey, when I began to live my life comparing myself to what others have and what others look like, I lost my way. I lost myself, I lost my identity, and I lost my authenticity. I no longer valued my opinion. Heck, I no longer trusted myself. Saddest of all, I lost sight of my dreams.

I began listening to the little voice in the dark space in my mind. I call it the "old nag." "You're dumb." "Your too fat." "You don't really think you are destined to be great, do you?" "Thank God for makeup because...."

I began looking for any reason to convince myself I was incapable of loving or being loved. I would berate myself until I came to believe I was an unworthy woman in whom God was severely disappointed.

I am "that girl" who showed up in life with a smile on my face; everyone thought I was such a happy person. I would say now that I was a "closet diver." I was acting happy during the day and drowning in despair in the silence and darkness of night. It was a survival technique, and it worked. Until the day it no longer did, and I wanted to walk away from life. It was in that moment of desperation that I picked up the phone and made a call to, as it turns out, the woman who would become my life/business coach and friend.

One of the first things I really owned was that, where you go, you follow. I can run as far away as I wanted; the truth is, no matter how hard I tried, I could not lose my shadow. Believe me; I have tried on more than one occasion.

It was one of those moments in life that I will never forget. Moments like where I was and what I was doing on 9/11, what the day was like when my children were born, or the day I graduated with my college degree that took me twenty-five years to complete. Those moments in life that

68

are so profound—when life takes a different path and a new life journey begins.

I was complaining, whining really, and pushing responsibility for myself onto other people.

"My family feels obligated to love me."

"My friends just like having me around, so they don't feel guilty about not inviting me."

"I am not smart. I just got very lucky on the test."

Worst of all, "God holds me to a much higher standard than He does anyone else. After all, I was in charge of His children as not only their teacher, but spiritual mentor as well; I was not living up to His standards. What a failure!"

Do you remember being in math class, and the assignment was to find the common denominator? Well, guess what? Finding the common denominator is not only for a math problem!

I was on the phone with my coach, pacing back and forth, in a state of complete despair, hopeless, dreamless, with no goals, verbally spewing excuse after excuse. All of a sudden, I blurted out, "Oh my God, I am the common denominator!"

I felt like I had run into a brick wall! The reality that I am absolutely the one responsible for sabotaging my own happiness and success was one of those life-altering moments I will never forget. No one is responsible for me but me. If I am responsible for the sabotaging, that must mean I am responsible for all the achievements as well.

BOOM!

The next moment, in typical coaching language, all I heard from my coach was, "Hmmm." So many emotions came together in an instant: sadness for not catching on sooner, joy for recognizing a life-changing event, excitement at what could lie ahead, and fear for, well, what could lie ahead for me. FEAR!

Fear paralyzes us from living a life we truly love and desire. What I learned about living a fearful life is that it is a survival technique. I am convinced I lived in fear of the world outside my bubble for so many decades because at least I knew I was alive; I was surviving. And that's good, right? Who doesn't want to survive? If I stepped in to the unknown, would I really be okay? It was much safer to avoid the urge to seek and explore than to take a chance something would go wrong.

I told myself over and over again: I am happy enough. I am a good enough. Besides, I don't really deserve to be happy, right? Because, after all, I am as happy as anyone else. That should be enough, right?

One of the most interesting conversations I have had over the past five years is that most everyone willing to talk about their own happiness and dreams feels the same way I felt.

I began talking responsibility for my actions, choices, and thoughts. Everything. No exceptions.

How did this shift of perspective happen for me? It did not happen overnight, but I can say it was the "I am the common denominator" statement that blew my eyes wide open. I began coaching with Stacey and taking classes in neuro-linguistic programming (NLP) that taught me to look at my values and beliefs and then embrace the same methods that individuals and organizations have used to get the outstanding results they set for themselves. Using NLP methodology has allowed me first to help myself and then to coach others to create the outcomes they want in their personal and/or professional lives.

I began taking responsibility for what the "old nag" was trying to accomplish and no longer allowed that voice to reign in my mind. I began being the friend to myself that I sought in others. I began planning a future where I was 100% involved in the planning and not just letting "nature takes its course."

At the young age of 51, I began designing a new direction in my life. I co-founded You.Empowered Services, LLC. It is my personal mission to change the world, one person at a time. I do this by asking people I meet, "How do you change the world?" Helping people realize that we all change the world by our careers, volunteering, parenting, loving, etc., one conversation at a time.

I met a young woman who, through research and training, has reduced the incidence of rape in Kenya. I met a young man who shows up every day at a job that pays very little, yet he takes it as his responsibility to make others smile and continues to dream his future. I met a man who, at 73, never thought about the fact that, as a CPA, he has kept people out of jail (that was actually really funny when I said that to him!). By helping others recognize their importance and significance, I contribute to a better world for each of us. It is one of my passions.

When the opportunities came up for me to purchase TEAM Referral Network in St. Louis, I took it. Despite having never professionally networked prior, I bought the franchise on a wing and a prayer. Between my husband's support and knowing that my coach would help me navigate building an organization that offers St. Louis business men and women the best opportunity to grow their businesses, I have begun building relationships among our members, resulting in connections made and businesses grown.

Yes, life happens and causes us pain. Tragedy strikes, and people move in and out of our life. How we choose to deal with it is up to us. It is incredibly humbling to hear someone say I coached them into a new outlook on their life, or a young man thanking me for a conversation that many will not have because of the color of his skin, or a friend met through networking who sends me a quick text saying they are so glad to call me "friend."

All these are gifts because I reached a point in my life where I said, "Enough is enough. I know there is more. There just has to be because I know I was not put here to play small, to live small, and to die small."

I look forward to my next 50 years of living a life of excellence! All because I quit comparing myself and realized I am perfect in who I am. I clearly understand that I have the power to change myself: If it's to be, it's up to me! (Thanks, BA, for that one!)

Derlene R Hirtz is on a personal mission to transform the world, one conversation at a time. We choose: be A change or be THE change. You Empowered Services coaches and offers training for professionals to grow and maximize strengths, reach potential, and achieve results never-before realized. Recognizing where we go, we follow, clients gain new tools that allow them to move past self-doubts and limiting decisions.

Derlene is also an inspiring and motivating speaker, certified NLP coach, certified trainer of NLP, and author of the book *Journey of Intention: Life Made to Order*. She is franchise owner of TEAM Referral Network in St. Louis, MO. She has earned the level of master practitioner in NLP and time line therapy. She holds a BA in education. She is a member of the National Speaker's Association and Toastmasters International.

Derlene is a grandmother, wife, mother, and friend. Her hobbies include riding her bike long distances, physical exercise, and playing with her twin granddaughters and her grandson.

Perception Is Everything
By Trudi Kayser

Several things in my life have made an impact on me.
Some events that specifically stick out will be shared in this
story. Their impact on me have helped me to impact others.
I was your typical small-town Southern girl, born in Paris,
Texas, and raised in an even smaller town called Blossom.
Paris and Blossom are referred to as "Tornado Alley." The
following incident made a major impact on my future
because of one decision.
I was almost 12. It was April 2, 1988. I heard my father
yelling at my mother and me to get out of the mobile home.
We ran outside, and what I saw next froze me in my tracks.
The tornado resulted from two other storms joining and
forming one large F5 tornado. We didn't realize what
damage it had left behind it. All we could think of was
getting to safety.

My parents were entrepreneurs; my father was a welder.
Before I was born, my parents owned a truck stop with a
restaurant attached. The building had long since been
burned in a fire but was still standing. It was a cinderblock
building with the insides gutted, a strong and a safe place to
seek refuge from a storm. My father was a collector of odd
items. He stored them inside this building. He was the
proud owner of two wheat combines. Both were in the
pathway of the tornado barreling down on us. It felt as
though everything was moving in slow motion. My father
told me to lay down on an old truck seat, and they hunkered
down by an old deep freezer inside the building.

It hit. It was the loudest, most obnoxious noise, and I
thought it would never stop. Tornados had come before, but
this one hit us! The wind was so bad, and my long hair was
being blown so hard it hurt my head. The building

75

collapsed, and the brick wall came tumbling down on me, but the seat folded over me and protected me. And as quickly as it began, it was over. It was eerily quiet. We stood up amid the wreckage, and we were surrounded by destruction. Looking up in the sky, the tornado had risen and was off to its next destination.

Trailer houses do not survive tornados. Nor do their contents. I played the piano, had for 3 years. I was the local church's piano player and had dreams of being a concert pianist. I had just been gifted a piano, and when I found it, it was destroyed. I thought, at that moment, I would never play again. I did later but was never excited about it. That day changed a lot of lives. That storm skipped across 3 states with dire consequences in every place it touched.

After the Red Cross came in and got people situated with places to stay, we pieced our lives back together with the rest of the town. My parents rented a camper trailer from a couple in the town next to ours. I found a wooden box in the camper trailer with Mexican jumping beans in it, and I kept it. It was the coolest thing in a world of crap. I had lost my animals, my piano, my home, and the facade of a family.

My mom and dad divorced, and I stayed with my mother. My dad moved to another state, and our lives went on. When I was 15 years old, I was working at a skating rink and met a guy. He was so good on roller skates, and all the girls wanted to date him. He was my first kiss. We dated, and it was a tumultuous relationship. One day, we were having a heart to heart about our relationship, and our conversation steered towards the tornado a few years before. He told me his parents had rented out their camper trailer to a couple in the next town, and when they got it back, his Mexican jumping beans were gone!

I was taken back. Could it be? I asked him a few questions, and we realized I had his beans! In our minds, it was a sign we were supposed to be together. We had been discussing parting ways. We stayed together for another 8 years and had 3 amazing children, the first of which we placed for adoption. My mother spiraled downhill even more with alcoholism after I married him, and I learned how to be the same and choose the same relationships she did as a young woman.

The 8-year marriage taught me some great lessons in life. That one decision, because of those beans, helped me to choose to lead a life as a drug addict and a manipulative maniac. I chose to be a victim.

Several failed relationships and my mother and father's death when I was very young left me feeling alone and empty in the world. When my husband and I separated, we attempted a few reconciliations; however, it never worked out. We had children and fought over them every chance we could.

The last time we were together, he took them, and I didn't see them for 8 years. That's another book! I got custody of them when they were 12 and 14. He was arrested for something too terrible to talk about in this story, and I was located by the police to be reunited with them. I had lived for 7 years, longing for my children. That time was filled with guilt and sadness, more anger and resentment. My story impacts others going through that now. The relationship I have with my children now is amazing. I was connected with the first born, Taylor, last year. He is 29 years old now!

That incident made a huge impact on my kids. I was in the middle of my addiction when I got them. The struggle of being a single mom with two very damaged children, who didn't like the mom who wasn't around while they were growing up, was enough to drive me to drink and do drugs more, not strive to get better.

After two years of hiding it and thinking I was succeeding, I finally decided to get sober.

On February 25, 2008, I went to AA and started changing my life. That was 9 ½ years ago and another marriage to the love of my life. So many things come to mind, and the one thing that sticks out the most is gratitude. The experiences I overcame and that made the most impact on me allowed me to become the person I am today. Over the past 9 years, I have diligently worked on myself. First in AA, with 14 sponsors and several people (you know who you are) who stuck by me through thick and thin to get me through those steps 4 times! AA was an amazing foundation to the life I have now.

I got tired of using the language being used and eventually stopped going at year 5. With great gratitude, I walked away from the meetings and program and informed my sponsors that I had learned a better way, using a modality that works for me. The mind is powerful when it's put to work using a new programming and not the ones instilled in it during childhood.

My mother's liver burst, and that's how she died when I was 26. She literally drank herself to death. Recently, I found out that every brother and sister I have is dead or dying from alcoholism. I was the youngest of 10. I broke the cycle! The women I helped in AA are still sober today. That's an amazing impact! The ripple effect it had on their families and friends is still felt to this day.

When I got sober, I was working for a beer distributor in San Diego, CA. Shortly after I entered recovery, the stock market crashed, and the following year, 200 of us were laid off. I took two years off and explored entrepreneurship. I was led by divine intervention to the career I am in now, and in recovery, I was able to accomplish what I only dreamed of years ago! I work with two amazing companies that believe in empowering individuals to make their own mark in this world. I was asked, when starting my career, what my goals were. I had no clue! I was then asked what I wanted my legacy to be. What footprint did I want to leave behind after I left this physical body?

I have always been one to care about the forward progress of others. Even as a child, it was prevalent. I didn't see it at the time, but hindsight is 20/20. Now, I see the impact I made on others growing up, mainly because they have told me. That question about my legacy got me to think about what life would be like for others, my children, my husband, and friends when I was gone from this physical body. I had no idea how overcoming struggles would inspire and create a passion in me that would lead to where I am and impact others the way it has.

Today, I educate others how to get through their money struggles in two ways. The name of my agency in the Phoenix area is Life Made to Order Financial – Phoenix, LLC. I teach individuals and businesses the 3 principles of saving and the 3 principles of protecting that money once they have saved it. We have workshops across the nation monthly and focus on women with our events called Wine, Women & Wealth. People want to be taught what to do with their finances, instead of told what to do. Our workshops and education empower individuals to do that. I also help small businesses and entrepreneurs grow through the power of relationship marketing with a company called TEAM Referral Networking. It's interesting that I specialize in that, considering my relationships were all one-sided and my money affairs were horrible. It all comes so naturally, and here is where the passion comes into play. I have learned that authenticity, being able to be myself always, no matter what, has sparked a passion and a purpose I had thought didn't exist.

One of the greatest compliments was given to me recently. A woman told me I was a powerful presence but in a humble way. The way I live my life is most important in creating impact in this world. I learned the hard way that children grow up to be adults, and the best way to teach and inspire is by example. My children didn't do what I told them to do. They did and repeated what I did as a young adult.

Today, I am elated to leave behind a legacy and impact others in a way that will ripple throughout their families. The lives I touch and the lessons others learn through my actions will prove that they, too, can be and do anything they set their minds to do. If a gutter addict that used to stick needles in her arms, lie, cheat, and steal from others can rise above and live this life I live now, anyone can!

Mindset is important in any endeavor we take on. My perception of my past has changed; my perception of my future has changed. My perception of our world has changed. Our thoughts are powerful. What are you creating right now with your thoughts?

Trudi Kayser lives and works in Phoenix, Arizona. She is an author, TEAM Referral Network area director, founder of Life Made to Order Financial – Phoenix, NLP practitioner, and time line therapist. After several years of alcohol and drug use, she turned her life around 10 years ago and strives to make an impact on everyone she meets. She uses the impact that life made on her to do so.

Ditching my Inner Straitjacket
By Naomi Calderon

A former personal trainer and yoga instructor, my scope of practice has evolved, and now, I work as a holistic nutrition and lifestyle coach. I am also a glitter-loving, medicine-bag-wearing, Converse-rocking woman. A delicious blend of Earth mama and city girl, my inner nerdy science girl is strong. Midwesterner by birth, but California girl at heart, I have a nomadic spirit and am married to a desert rat, who likes to stay put.

Often, people assume that, given my years in the health and fitness industry, I grew up health conscious. Nothing could be further from the truth! If it had been up to me, the 5 food groups would have been the following: Cake, Cookies, Candy, Pie, Ice cream.

Thankfully, my mom was smart enough not to let me be in charge of meal planning.

At 17—long before it became widely understood—I was diagnosed with candida. My allergist put me on what felt like an incredibly restrictive diet. While, physically and mentally, I felt so much better, emotionally, I felt deprived and punished.

Shortly before that diagnosis, I was sexually assaulted. I hid it for years, while slut-shaming myself into silence. It must have been my fault, or so I believed. I saw myself as "damaged goods."

These two things came together in the perfect storm that fostered years of believing I didn't deserve the yummy things in life because I was broken.

I did a great job at hiding it all, shoving down the guilt, shame, and judgement. On the outside, my life looked pretty good. Inside, I was a tangled mess of fear, self-loathing, and anger.

Honestly, I thought no one knew. I did my best to hide the mess and keep it locked down. I didn't want people to know the truth. I thought they, too, would see me as broken. Hiding it all was my way of controlling the situation, from my own emotions to people's perceptions of me.

In my early 30s, I was engaged, and 2 months before the wedding, my fiancé told me he was falling in love with someone else.

So, there I was, carrying around this guilt and shame, believing I must somehow deserve to be deprived. With his pronouncement, I topped it off with a huge pile of "I'm unlovable."

It was obvious to me I was not enough. I was depressed, overweight, and thought that was simply my lot in life.

Sometime after that split, I happened upon a book about real people making extraordinary changes—physically, mentally, emotionally—through a nutrition and exercise challenge. These were "regular" people, not those who grew up athletically inclined. Just your average Joe's. It lit a spark of hope. So, I decided to start it. In secret. Because, what if it didn't work?

I faithfully used the little gym in our work complex. The craziest thing happened. I started seeing results! That created feelings of accomplishment and an outward appearance of confidence, which lit a fire to take it a step further. So, I hired a trainer and learned all I could from him. Together, we completely re-shaped my physique.

The first time I had to go into the gym without him (he worked out of a Gold's Gym), I panicked. I broke a sweat before I even crossed the threshold. The gym was filled with a bunch of seasoned gym rats and a smattering of pretty people. I felt completely out of my element, and the "not enough" monster showed up like some big hulking beast, ready to consume me whole. I came close to turning around and leaving.

In that moment, I decided I wanted to help other women who were too afraid to start because they didn't know what they were doing. So, I pulled up my gym socks and marched inside. Afterwards, I started studying for my personal training certification.

I spent 5 years on the fitness side of the wellness industry as a personal trainer and yoga instructor.

It was the yoga mat that began to crack me open. Initially, I attacked it the same way I did my gym workouts. I was going to master the mat.

That had been my approach to my fitness routine. I. Controlled. It. All. The food, the workouts. All of it. My friends thought I was nuts. I simply said I was dedicated.

Being committed to my health through my workouts and eating healthy was good. It was the underlying motivation that created an unhealthy practice. That was about control. Forcing my body to comply. I believed, if I looked a certain way, maybe then I would magically become lovable.

Yoga challenged my control monster. Dropping into my body on the mat provided the access to long-buried emotions that I needed to feel, that needed to come up and out.

Emotions get "trapped" in our bodies, and there were times that certain poses tapped into those emotions in a way that 2 years of therapy never had. I would find myself sobbing on the mat, emotionally spent.

That was when my healing began.

My time on the mat helped me to learn not to hold on to control quite so tightly. Yet, I felt like there was a piece missing. Much like when I hired my trainer, I eventually hit a plateau. Then, I was introduced to a life and spiritual coach. I dove into her year-long program, excited finally to begin living.

At that time, I was also working with a couple of amazing healers and mentors. I attended my first Inipi ceremony (what people refer to as a sweat lodge).

Through the spiritual practices I learned and began following, I was able to face that past I was so afraid of. It allowed me to begin releasing those old emotions, the negative things I was using to hold myself hostage, and finally to see myself in a new light.

I stopped hiding and haven't had a candida flare up since. (Did I mention, emotionally speaking, candida is all about hiding?)

There are so many things I've learned from being a student and in my role as the teacher and coach. There are 3 that stand out. They are what I share with clients and what I sometimes go back and remind that 16-year-old me who was afraid to face the world.

Be unapologetically you.
Embrace your goofy side. Rock the Converse. Revel in the LBD. Whatever makes you sparkle, shine, light up, and feel free.

What people say is really about them, not about you. Let. That. Shit. Go. YOU get to define yourself!

Do what makes you happy and shine your brilliant light. In this moment, in this time, the world would be incomplete without you in it.

Mistakes.
It's all how you look at them. Rather than making yourself wrong, simply approach them from the standpoint of "what worked, what didn't work, and what do I want to do differently next time." I have found that, by reframing mistakes as simply a decision that didn't work [how you expected] or worked until it didn't, rather than wrong or bad or any other harsh judgmental crap, you will be well on your way to creating life, not just surviving it.

Set boundaries.
Use your voice. Say no. Ask for what you want. (It's ok to want what you want. Really.) For anyone else who has battled with that "I'm not enough" monster, that one bears repeating out loud.

Sometimes, it even means setting boundaries with yourself.

Recently, someone asked if I was where I thought I'd be when I was a kid. Not even close. If I had pursued my childhood dreams, I'd be a flute-playing ballerina, and I like what I'm doing.

I gone from "unlovable" to married to a man who thinks I am the bees' knees. (That's good, in case you've not heard that phrase.) Shifting that took breaking me open, being willing to look in the dark corners at all the things I was afraid to face—all the crap I had shoved down and buried, while judging myself incredibly harshly. It required me to open up to love—romantic and otherwise.

I trust myself more.

I needed to be willing to be open, vulnerable, and get the coaching. Learning from others was the biggest gift I could've ever given myself. It has been part of what has shaped how I work with clients today.

I needed that time in the gym and on the mat to understand the physical aspects of a healthy lifestyle. I discovered clients who were willing to talk about what they were doing in the kitchen, got better results than those who didn't. Those willing to talk about food AND what was going on emotionally got the BEST results.

That spurred the evolution of my career from trainer to holistic nutrition and lifestyle coach. A lifelong learner, I strove to hone my coaching and healing skills even further and completed certifications as master practitioner of NLP and integrated time line therapy.

Working with clients is an honor and privilege. I've been blessed to work with some amazing individuals. One former client I trained 10 years ago recently shared this with me:

"Thanks, Naomi. My passion, because of you, has been to help people get fit. You changed my life, and I have been able to help others with gastric (bypass). It's an untapped industry. Working with you was the best investment I ever made…and I gained a friend!"

My belief is this: we each have it in us to thrive.

I help clients to take the crisis out of midlife. To live true to their passions and to ditch the cultural constructs of "busy is better." It's time to stop buying into the fraud of busy and ignoring inner emotional dialogue.

Now is the time to honor who you are, all the parts and pieces, shadow side and light. No judgement, no shame. All a celebration.

My mission is to impact positively the health of the next 7 generations by improving the health and wellness of today.

So, when a client—a mom of a special needs teenager—goes from locking herself in her room 3-4 days at a time, 2-3 times a month to homeschooling her son, exercising 5x/week, no more depression, rash on her face gone, and landing a job she LOVES…that makes my heart sing. I know I'm fulfilling my mission.

Before my friend John crossed over, I remember him looking at me and saying, "Stop taking life so seriously. It's all just a big joke anyway."

He didn't mean life was a joke and not to care. Just the opposite. That it was an adventure, an experiment of sorts, and that getting wrapped up in stress and control misses the point of life completely.

John held the wisdom of the universe. I continue to remind myself to let go of the need to control and to drop into the experience. It is in those moments that true freedom exists. Letting go of the need to hide and control loosened the straitjacket I had created for myself. Now, my mission is to embody health and to live from a place of freedom and to help others learn how to do the same for themselves.

"The only way to deal with an unfree world is to become so absolutely free that your very existence is an act of rebellion." - Albert Camus

As a former personal trainer and a yoga instructor, I bring the "drop and give me 20!" attitude of the gym together with the "oooohm" of yoga to my coaching sessions. My deep belief is that simple is the new sexy and that we all have it in us to thrive. I'm committed to untangling the mess that is the conversation about health and nutrition to help clients discover easy-peasy ways to live—and eat—with more vitality.

During my time in the health and wellness field, I've had the good fortune to work with clients and groups at public and private institutions, including Google, Yahoo! and AOL. I'm a member of the American Association of Drugless Practitioners and committed to working with clients through whole foods.

My Life
By Laurie Hance

I'm not sure there were large moments in my life that were defining. It was more like hundreds of small moments that made subtle shifts in my life that, over time, were like compound interest and led to major changes and growth. For example, in the late 90s, I was working at a small office and took walks with a woman from a neighboring office during our lunch breaks. This person was several years older and in charge of an alcohol rehab program. One time on a walk, after listening to me rant about how awful my life was, etc., she asked me when I was going to stop being a victim. I was not sure I understood her. She did her best to explain what she meant. I wasn't quite ready to hear it, but it's something I remember, and although I can't attach specific changes in my life to that moment, I know it had an impact. It was most likely a reminder to my subconscious that I needed to wake up.

Another moment was when, during that same job, I was fired and told I should find work that is less detail-oriented. Well, details were not my problem; my problem was boredom. This pushed me to think constantly about my career and to consider a career, rather than a good job. I started looking at options, talking to people, and trying to figure things out. One day while driving, I remembered that I had always enjoyed doing massage and had wanted to be a physical therapist when I grew up. My time in the Army proved to me that I didn't want to be in the medical world, but massage therapy was different, and that wasn't a highly detailed job or career. I found a school that worked for me and around my work schedule. This choice had a huge impact on my life. For the first time since high school, I started an education program and actually finished it.

The connections I made in massage school impacted my life. I met my friend Deborah, who became a co-facilitator for a yearlong priestess spiritual growth program. Through this program, I took part in ceremonies, such as re-birth, death, marriage to my masculine side, writing my story and releasing the hold it had on me. The ceremonies had an impact on me and allowed for the shifts I was ready to receive.

The growth and confidence I gained from this program led me to the decision to take charge of my health and to have weight-loss surgery. All the little decisions that came to weight-loss surgery led me to make new friends, start hiking, biking, running, and become the more outgoing person I knew I was inside. I began loving myself more at this point and wanting more for myself. This triggered the desire for a better career or something that was more meaningful. I still didn't know what I wanted, but I did know what I didn't want. I still had some of that lingering doubt about being detail-oriented, regardless of the fact that I had been succeeding at a detailed job for several years. This led me to my next step.

While I attended massage therapy school, and later, when I had the weight-loss surgery, I was employed at the same company. Within the first week I was there, I knew this was the wrong place for me. I stayed on because my husband was unemployed, we had just failed in our first business doing signs and banners, and I had lost my job. We needed an income more than I needed to be comfortable. I was there 11 years, and although there were aspects of what I did that I enjoyed, the company morale and personality were just not a fit for me.

I often looked at other jobs, but they were just more of the same. I knew I didn't want what I already had. At one point, I started getting calls from recruiters with insurance companies. I was intrigued by being a business owner and finally being able to make the money I felt I should, considering how hard I always worked. I wasn't ready to take that leap, since it was commission only, and I knew it would be hard to survive in the first several months. So, I didn't take the leap; in fact, I didn't do anything. I just got more miserable at work the more things changed and the next generation in the family-owned business came on board.

Their personalities were so different from me and so toxic to the company that I wanted to leave more than ever. Yet, I had no clue what I wanted to do, and the 2008 recession had scared me so much that I was afraid to let go of what I had.

The decision was made for me when my position was "restructured," and I was laid off. It was the blessing I needed in my life.

I started looking for work and was again approached by insurance companies. This time, I researched and decided to make the leap. I was on unemployment and could collect while I got things started with the business.

I didn't grow up knowing anything about insurance and would have told you that sales and insurance were not something I would do. The universe brings us what we want and what we need. I wanted independence, freedom, unlimited earning potential, and a sense of pride. That's what I receive with this career.

My biggest obstacles have been my own ego and lack of self-esteem or self-love. My friends and family have always encouraged me and loved me. I didn't love myself or see the value I brought the world and how my gifts, not that I recognized that I had any, could impact the world or be something of value that others would want.

I didn't allow myself to follow my dreams; in fact, I shut off my dreams. I stopped looking for things I wanted and goals to go for. I was on autopilot, just floating along.

Today, I want to write and publish books that reach kids on an unconscious level to help them stay connected to their inner selves. Kids naturally believe in themselves and focus on the good or positives in their life. Then, as we age and we start caring what society thinks and comparing ourselves to others and get limiting beliefs ingrained in us, we start giving up on our dreams and start thinking that what someone else thinks about us is more important than what we think. At this point, we are so disconnected to our inner self, our inner voice, that we stop listening. When we stop listening, we no longer see all the amazing possibilities there are, and we stop seeing the connections that are there to make the beautiful things happen.

I want to help future generations avoid the hang-ups I've experienced by focusing on the lack of money, lack of opportunities, lack of intelligence, lack of self-esteem and self-love and simply not believing they are, capable of doing or becoming whatever they want. I hope, through my stories, I can help them stay on the track they connect with on some level. Simple reminders to use empowering language and stories that give them a sense that the universe is there for them and wants to see them succeed.

I would love to say I would give myself some great advice so my life would have been easier, but that would mean I wouldn't be who I am today. It has been my challenges that have made me who I am today, and I would be a different person if I made changes. Additionally, my younger self was simply not ready for the lessons I am getting and

94

learning today. If I had been told about following the universe's guide and trusting my unconscious mind when I was 18 years old, I would have thought you were nuts. That's crazy talk. So, until I experienced certain events and saw specific things, I wasn't ready for those learnings.

With that said, I would like to show my younger self how much I am loved. I have struggled with self-love most of my life, and if I could accept my own love and see my own internal power and beauty, my growth and changes could have been so much sooner.

I would tell my 27-year-old self to invite her parents to her wedding. My husband and I eloped, even though we didn't need to. Both our parents loved our choice in a partner. I had never had the dreams that most girls did when they were little about a big wedding with the fancy dress and all the romantic stuff. I just knew I would get married, and I was happy with that. It was his second marriage, so he didn't have any desire to have a big wedding. We ran off and eloped and planned on having a wedding for the family later. Instead, we purchased a home. I should have asked my parents to take a last-minute trip to Las Vegas. I didn't realize until afterwards that, just because I didn't dream of a wedding ceremony, that others didn't dream of it for me. I hurt my parents, and that is the biggest thing I regret. That would be something I would love to be able to give myself advice on.

I think the impact I have had on myself has been to allow myself to love me for who I am and to embrace who I am. By being myself and focusing on the positive and expecting others to do the same, I feel I can offer those same subtle shifts to people who are ready to experience them.

Some people have massive changes in their life or catastrophic events that force change on them. Many others do not have those earth-shattering events. I have made drastic changes in my life one subtle shift at a time, one day at a time, and one new connection at a time. I now see how one small decision triggers the next, which triggers the next, which triggers the next. All this synchronicity impacts our lives and makes huge impacts. We just don't see the changes because they are so small at each step. So, if I could impress one thing, it would be to ask you to look at the little things in your life that have changed and follow the pattern. From there, you can focus on the future and believe that your goals and desires along that line of synchronicity will fall into place. Just keep moving forward and expect that all is falling into place for you.

I have lived in the Inland Empire since 1994. I moved to California when I finished my time as a combat field medic in the US Army. I got married in 1997 and we currently have three fur babies. I am originally from a small rural town in Oregon where I spent my entire youth up until graduating high school. I moved to the outskirts of Portland, OR, and attended Mt Hood Community College where I studied journalism.
I am an aspiring writer and currently own my own insurance agency. I still offer mobile massage services for a select handful of clients.

Back from the Abyss
By Cindy Logan

730 evaluation…. Most people don't know what that is! I know I didn't prior to 2004. I have a friend who is a psychiatrist. He said: "If you want to mess up your children, get a divorce. If you REALLY want to cause emotional scars, do a 730 evaluation."

In 2004, my ex-husband attempted to gain custody of our children, who were 14 and 15. To do that, he tried to prove me unfit as a mother, taking me back to court and requiring a 730 evaluation to take away my parental rights.

The legal definition, taken directly from the Family Code, is as follows:

> Courts order child custody evaluations, investigations, and assessments to assist them in determining the health, safety, welfare, and best interest of children with regard to disputed custody and visitation issues. This rule governs both court-connected and private child custody evaluators appointed under Family Code section 3111, Evidence Code section 730, or Code of Civil Procedure section 2032.

The reality is brutal: 8 months of being under a microscope. Tests… Personality test, psychological test. Assessments… Job assessment, mental health assessment, other skills assessments, PARENTING assessments.

Taking my children to the psychologist, seeing their pain. Hearing them say, with pain in their voice, "No, I don't want to live with my dad." Feeling their pain, feeling helpless, persecuted. Unable to work, unable to build my business. My agency, which was thriving before the 730 evaluation, dwindled and eventually died.

The world became a dark, scary place for me, where I was doing the right thing and being persecuted. I watched the father of my children attempt to devalue me. I heard truths, partial truths, and outright lies directed at me. He knew all my buttons. He knew my mother and my brothers and sisters had lost custody of their children.

I had helped him build his business, using our savings, working, using my 401k, using the equity in the house to finance his business. As a life coach, with an undergrad in business and a master's degree in management, I coached him and watched his business go from $60K to $120K to $250k in 18 months. When it reached $250k, he left, leaving behind the start-up costs for his business, called a 30-year mortgage, which was twice the mortgage we attained to buy the house. And I felt like a failure. Even with all the successes I had facilitated, I made his choice about me and decided I couldn't coach anymore.

As I was building my agency, he filed the 730, giving me upset, two daughters in need of massive emotional support and extra time, and causing great heartache.

I

       SANK

            DEEP

                  DEEP

                      DEEP into a depression.

I won the case. First, the psychologist said I was a fit mother. The personality test proved it. Then, the mediator said the same thing. Then finally, the judge ruled. Each time, he kept going. Even when the judge ruled in my favor, based on the psychological report, he said he would take it to court. With each "win," I was elated. Then, as he persisted, I became more deflated, feeling even more persecuted, not trusting anyone, not even trusting myself. After all, I had picked Mike as the father of my children. Clearly, my picker was broken!

I did not realize I was in a depression until years later. In 2009, I woke up. However, it was like the groundhog on February 2, Groundhog Day. I popped my head up, saw my life in shambles. My house was unrecognizable, and I realized I had been in a depression. And, I immediately went back into my hidey hole. The last day I spent in bed, unable to move, was 2012, several years later.

From 2012, life started improving. However, I had gotten myself in such a horrible financial state, I saw no hope of coming back from it. I first took a position as a TEAM Referral Network director, building chapters in San Diego, working with my coach, Stacey O'Byrne. This eased my financial burden a little. I went from a negative financial position to a 0. Zero looked great when, the year before, everything looked unmanageable. I then took a position with a national real estate investor education company that flew me around the country for their 3-day seminars. I made great money; however, they overbuilt and had to let people go.

In 2014, tragedy struck in my family. I had to make a decision to keep my house or keep my daughter alive. I rarely worked for the next 3 years. It took a year to sell the house, using a short payoff, meaning I didn't receive proceeds from the sale. I owed more than the house was worth. That is another story and is covered in my book *The Five-Week Formula to a Better Brain*.

So, today, I do real estate out of state, where people can invest and have positive cashflow. My clients appreciate that I have introduced them to a group that can be trusted. My Power Teams have duplicatable systems that allow them to find cash-flowing properties in 4 distinct markets. I build chapters for TEAM Referral Network, bringing together entrepreneurs to build their business through relationship marketing.

And I'm coaching again. I'm using NLP (neuro-linguistic programming) and timeline therapy that allows my clients to make great strides in their lives. I help people get out of their own way, showing them how they can be even more successful, how they can take their business to the next level.

All my businesses are about improving lives. Improving financial lives, getting individuals set for retirement through creating cashflow with real estate. Improving business lives, putting together referral groups. Improving personal lives, facilitating breakthroughs to set people free from the bondage of past baggage.

Looking back on my life, if I could talk to my younger self, I would give her an earful!

This may sound a little cynical, and it is what it is. Financially, DON'T co-mingle assets; keep your assets separate. Use a loan for start-up costs, where all the interest is tax deductible. Don't sell assets in a community property state, where the funds are then co-mingled. And DO have a pre-nuptial agreement so you can protect yourself.

Emotionally, know that people will make their own decisions, based on their own baggage. And they may blame you and probably will. Keep yourself CLEAR, knowing it is THEIR stuff. Know that you are someone who makes a difference. You elevate people. Use food as nutrition; don't turn to food and drink when emotionally drained.

Stay in integrity; walk in the light and you will feel better about yourself.

Trust yourself.

Ask for help, lean on others, and allow them to support you. Keeping your chin up and pretending all is well when it isn't serves no one. Being a lone ranger serves no one. And, when you ask for help, you can get the change you need. You have amazing friends who are coaches, hypnotherapists, and great resources. Work with someone who can get you out of a funk! You can make more of a difference in the world when you are being your best self.

Looking back on my life, I have made a huge impact for so many. I joined the Army at 17 and was promoted early for every rank. I received the Good Conduct Medal and the Army Commendation Medal. I was the only one in my family to graduate high school and the first in my extended family to graduate college. I inspired many with my story of escaping an abusive situation and thriving, both in the Army and in college.

I became a coach in my 30s, helping my now ex-husband go from $60K to $120K to $250K in 18 months. I helped a soccer coach quadruple his income in one month, and I helped a telemarketer, on notice he would be fired, go to receiving awards within 3 months. I helped many others, but those 3 stand out because their transformation was so dramatic.

I went into retirement at 35 and volunteered in my daughters' schools, in my church, in my community, and as a coach.

Going forward, I have even more impact to make. Completing and publishing my book, *The 5-Week Formula to a Better Brain,* will allow individuals to become sharper, more focused, and have more fun in their lives. The catalyst for that book is also not in this story. However, even though the book is not published yet, I have helped my friends change their emotional state. Creating a 5-week seminar or webinar will assist participants in creating more focus, changing their state, and managing their self-talk. Getting re-grounded financially will allow me to make even more of an impact with others' finances. In 2015, I sold my personal home, although I had other houses out of state. In 2017, I bought my personal home again, the first foundational step in financial independence. I bought my first home when I was 20, so it is a joy to be back to homeownership.

As I continue to develop my NLP skills, I can see how my clients can move forward with velocity.

I have much work to do, and I'm very excited to do it! I am someone who makes a difference!

Cindy Logan joined the Army at 17 to escape an abusive situation. She was the only one in her family to graduate high school and went on to get a master's degree in management from University of California. She has had a lifelong commitment to making a difference.

She became a coach in her 30s, effecting tremendous impact on the lives of her clients. What she hears most from her friends and clients is that they are so happy to have met her because she has changed their lives! She has a gift to see the potential an individual has.

Cindy is resilient, bouncing back from challenges. In her book, *Five Weeks to a Better Brain*, she shows you how to have more fun, more focus and more action in your life.

You Can Go Now
By Jordon Wolan

I was born into an upper middle-class Jewish family in
Long Island. Dad was a successful gynecologist and Mom
just wanted a normal girl. What my family ended up with
was a hypnotherapist, breakthrough coach and Reiki master
who talks a lot about energy and occasionally shows them
some odd demonstration of how to suspend someone
between two chairs. They still have no idea what I do.

Until the summer of my fifth year, I was a "normal girl."
Born to swim, I spent most of my days at the local pool, or
running around with the other kids, playing tennis,
pretending to be unicorns, and climbing trees. A bad day
was when the ice cream cart was out of cherry Italian ices.
Life was good. Then my skin started changing.

Small white spots appeared in contrast to my very tan arms
and legs. As the white patches grew, so did the staring, and
other kids began to ask me if I had been in a fire. There was
no more hiding it.

I finally received the diagnosis: vitiligo, a disorder in which
the immune system attacks and destroys the pigment-
producing cells (melanocytes) in the skin. Symmetrical or
asymmetrical patches of skin become lighter or turn white.
There is no cure and the only known treatment was to
choke down large green pills and then stand in a UV light
box for twenty minutes at the dermatologist's office several
days a week. I also was told that it was probably best to
avoid all activities involving sunlight.

While other kids still looked forward to going to the pool, I
suffered under new anxieties, clutching my tube of
sunscreen and hiding under towels. Summers became

traumatic, as I dreaded having to wear shorts or pose for photos on vacation. When people would ask what happened to my arms, I would explain but shrink inside. No, I hadn't been burned in a fire. It wasn't painful, and it wasn't contagious. I felt ugly and out of control no matter how much family told me I was beautiful. I could pretend that I was pretty for a while, but the moment I saw my spots in the photos, the illusion would be broken.

Middle school was the worst of it, and I spent hours alone, writing, and was always the quietest one in class. I began therapy for social anxiety. My parents thought it would help me come out of my shell, but it may have reinforced that there was something "wrong" with me. I would watch the Hans Christian Anderson movie from the 70s starring Danny Kaye, with the story of the ugly duckling. I yearned for the day when I would turn into the swan. When would it happen?

In the meantime, I did what any young girl in the same situation might do: I took up team sports and martial arts. By the time I graduated high school, I had never gone on a date but had a black belt, a muscular physique, shelves of awards and trophies, and knew how to incapacitate someone eight different ways. I had given up on the idea of ever growing into a beautiful swan that someone could love, and for my sweet sixteen, my mom hired a dozen Merchant Marines to attend as dates for my friends. I was okay with that.

Disaster struck again. I began to have feelings about other women and didn't know what was going on; no one talked about those things, then. With my identity thrown into further confusion, depression set in. I began to search for myself through relationships with both genders, leaving a trail of mixed signals and heartbreak. Every person I dated, male or female, represented something I wanted that might help me see who I was, but I never felt good about myself. In every relationship, I felt like I was changing my skin all over again.

It is said that every relationship acts as a mirror allowing us to see—and know—ourselves more clearly. I eventually found one that would shatter.

Fast-forward: I was in a long-term relationship. Though deeply in love with my partner, we were dealing with some heavy challenges that neither of us were equipped to handle. While they struggled with the past and finding wholeness, I could see only a future where the past could no longer hold me back. I had attended a transformational weekend seminar, and the awakening I had in that room was as close as I've ever felt to enlightenment. I understood that we all had stories, and I realized the extent of my full responsibility to create my reality. It left me ready to take on the world.

However, I didn't yet have the tools to help me wield my new sense of power and purpose. I was with the person I loved, still so stuck in the old story and reality. I was pulled in different directions by my efforts to hold both of us together. In the beginning of the relationship, I had seen my partner as my savior; by the end of it, I was trying to be theirs. Ignoring the warning signs that I was losing myself, I was barely eating and sleeping, and suffering under health problems. I had isolated myself from my friends and family. I eventually lost my job, and my home with my partner felt like a war zone. After a few more years, everything I had loved and known had dissolved around me, and I was emotionally numb and exhausted.

One cold night, riding my motorcycle on the freeway, I heard the very loud thought, "You can go now." I had a very clear image of driving myself into the truck in front of me. My mind then went eerily quiet, and I felt a sensation as though it was beginning to crack. I knew it was time to get help.

I enrolled in a Reiki class. The idea of learning a method of healing comforted me, making me feel connected to my dad, the doctor. And I thought, "Well, at least I'll be able to do something useful that might help someone else."

In Reiki class, we worked on learning to feel energy flowing between our hands, and the first time I felt it, I knew things were going to be okay. In that moment, I noticed a giant crow perched outside the classroom window. He might have been looking for a snack, but I took it as a sign. I didn't have all the answers yet, and it wasn't up to me to heal anyone else. I knew through this practice, I would learn how to heal myself.

I also began seeing a hypnotherapist, which would change the course of my life. In her office, I felt peace and hope. After all my years in psychotherapy, hypnosis was a new experience. I finally woke up. I'd already ended that difficult relationship, and now I regained self-esteem and confidence, working through my most severe trauma. It worked fast! I had things to do! I found my strength and realized that I could become a hypnotherapist myself and be able to do for others what she had done for me, which was to give me back my life.

For the next year, hypnotherapy college was my home. I threw myself into the study of the unconscious mind. Life was not about luck and waiting for things to change but about visualizing outcomes and rewiring old habits to make new ones. In one year, I had overcome my fear of public speaking and been interviewed twice on Hypnosis TV. I'd also used my new drive to become a Reiki master and even had students of my own.

I gravitated toward the work of others I'd encountered in my studies. Milton Erickson's use of metaphors and hypnotic language patterns to help his clients fascinated me. The martial artist in me saw neuro-linguistic programming like Erickson's hypnotherapy as mental jujitsu, used as a defense from the parts of yourself that seek to instill self-doubt. Subconscious Self-Defense for Self-Mastery—nice tagline! I immersed myself in the study of NLP, which felt to me like Disneyland for the mind. Eight months later, I was a trainer, the ultimate proof that I could achieve anything I decided to do.

I was a bit of a geek and hungry for transformation. I don't expect others to throw themselves as readily into hardcore transformation, sitting in a freezing conference room facing a practitioner for ten hours. That's all fun and games to me, for sure, but the clients I began to see were regular business people, moms, students, athletes—people who needed help with writer's block or fear of needles, who wanted to stop smoking, lose weight, make more sales calls, or end a toxic relationship. While I've noticed that this kind of healing attracts people who are visionaries and high achievers, passionate and persistent enough to play full out, it's for anyone who just wants help getting out of their own way, just like I did.

Finally, I started my own practice, calling it Life Activation Therapies, so I could devote my life to helping others heal. Through all of this, I was continuing to heal myself. For a person who used to be comfortable being invisible, I had achieved every goal I set, and people knew who I was.

So, you might be wondering: what happened with the duckling and the swan?

One day, while looking in the mirror, I noticed that except for my arms, my body was almost completely depigmented, my vitiligo barely noticeable. I realized people were probably confused when I spoke about how I "looked different." To my surprise, I felt a bit of sadness in that moment, as if the story that I'd been carrying around all those years was no longer relevant to me.

If I could go back and talk to my former self, that thirteen-year-old who believed that no one would ever see her as beautiful because of her spots, I would tell her this: just wait. It's going to be okay to stand out, to be different. There are other kids like you. You're going to see this as a strength someday. In 2012, I had an idea to reach kids like that thirteen-year-old.

I organized a photography project called "More Than My Skin." I put out a call to my tribe, found them, and we did photo shoots in downtown LA together. Over the next few years, around the world, through the ease of social media, a worldwide movement had sprung up. Vitiligo was becoming visible through projects like mine, on blogs, YouTube, websites, through models, support groups, conferences. Suddenly, our spots were cool. The group that was born of "More Than My Skin" had morphed into So Cal Vitiligo, and we still hold events. We hold space for our tribe to find us.

What I've learned is to see being uncomfortable as a positive thing. It can still feel at times like I'm alone and no one will understand, but that changes the moment I speak from my heart, through the fear. Feeling uncomfortable means that I am stretching and becoming someone I've never been before. It's why my life's work is to help other people do the same. Many people just want to feel good enough, as though that's the best they can do. My hope for them is more. My hope is for every beautiful swan who believes they are broken to find wholeness again.

Jordan Wolan is a breakthrough coach and certified hypnotherapist. Jordan's interest in results-oriented healing therapies stemmed from her own experiences with hypnotherapy, NLP, and time line therapy. Her personal experiences motivated her to help individuals and groups from a diverse array of backgrounds.

She is a certified trainer of NLP and a master practitioner of integrated time line therapy, as well as a Reiki master/teacher.

In 2012, she founded So Cal Vitiligo, which continues to host events several times a year. Originally from New York, Jordan now lives in LA with a very bitey cat named Jade, and she hasn't eaten kettle corn in almost three years thanks to NLP. She has been a competitive martial artist and athlete, and she practices the art of fire spinning in her free time.

IMPACT THROUGH GIVING
By Kelli C. Holmes

I remember it like it was yesterday, sitting at my dining room table with my assistant, Rayleen. It was June, 2002. I was VERY pregnant with my second child, Charlotte. Rayleen and I were working on developing the programs and systems that would soon become TEAM Referral Network.

I excitedly told Rayleen of my goal: "We will donate a membership to a local non-profit or charity that works with children and families in EVERY chapter of TEAM!"

The non-profits would become members and share their organization's mission with this dynamic group of business owners from the community, who would then become advocates for their organization. We know business owners and entrepreneurs WANT to give back to their community, but sometimes they don't know where, how, or what to do to achieve this. However, if we build the giveback INTO their marketing and growing of their business, we could create significant impact into the community and have it be a win-win!

As I was explaining my vision to Rayleen, I could see giving away hundreds and hundreds of memberships to local charities and how this would have such a positive effect on the charities and on the members too, as they would feel so good about helping them. At that moment, I could feel the potential impact this could have on the world...

To which Rayleen, ever the VOR (voice of reason), said, "That's great, Kelli, but before we go giving away hundreds and hundreds of TEAM memberships, can we get our first chapter up and running?"

So much has happened since June of 2002, and today, I am so happy to say we have donated hundreds of memberships in TEAM to some incredible non-profits!

Here are a few highlights:

Over the years, we have hosted many events to benefit our non-profit members of TEAM. One of my favorites has always been TEAM Referral Network's Annual Charity Golf Tournament and Mixer. Those who like to build relationships and help out worthy causes golf and those who just like to party with a cause mix! (And there are those who like both!) In recent years, we have had many NFL alumni play with us. Our events have raised over $100,000 for the benefit of our non-profit TEAM members.

Sometimes, it's the small things that make an impact…like the time a local boys' home, the McKinley Children's Center, received a donation of 25 fresh-cut Christmas trees to decorate their cottages and send out to foster families. Unfortunately, liability issues required that McKinley's fire-retard the trees and provide stands with water bowls. This was an expense the charity couldn't afford; it just wasn't in the budget. But one phone call from a person involved in TEAM had a local tree farm picking up the trees from the home, taking them to the farm to fire-retard them and affix with tree stands. They then delivered the trees back to the home, ready for distribution and decoration!

Some of our non-profit members have even claimed their membership in TEAM has helped them keep their doors open and has helped projects and services that may not have been able to happen without the help of their TEAM chapter members. This was particularly important during the years of the recession when much of the funding they relied on dried up.

Sometimes, you are so busy handling your daily business that you don't realize the profound effect you are making in the world. Around 2011, I was invited by then TEAM Director Terilee Harrison and TEAM member Marlia Cochran to be a guest on their show Elevate Radio. The theme of the show was about giving. They asked me to share information about TEAM's Community Outreach Program.

Both Terilee and Marlia were members of TEAM at the time. During the interview, Terilee opened up about participating in an event with her chapter's non-profit, the Soroptimist Club. The event took place in August at the start of the school year. They had teamed up with the local school district who brought in children by bus to the local Target store. The school had identified children in need. Each child brought a wish list that specified their clothing sizes. They "teamed up" an adult with a child or two, gave them a budget to spend and a limited time to go shopping.

Terilee shared how much it meant to her to take her assigned 9-year-old girl shopping. She helped her to buy underwear, socks, shoes, an outfit, and a backpack—all the things she needed and wouldn't have had if it hadn't been for the generous work of this non-profit. She went on to say that if she hadn't been a member of TEAM, she would have never been able to experience such a special time helping this young girl.

I remember thinking at the time how I had not really thought about the profound impact we could have on our TEAM members too. I had always focused on the positive effect we could have on the non-profits. Hearing her story brought tears to my eyes and even more meaning to what we get to do every day in our TEAM chapters with this program.

GIVING BACK IS IMPORTANT TO US

A significant part of TEAM Referral Network's mission is to "positively impact our member's businesses and the community to which they belong." Because community is so important to who we are, our network seeks to provide opportunities for our chapters and members to give back. Our passion is to positively impact hundreds of charities and non-profits where we have a TEAM chapter.

The TEAM Referral Network achieves this community focus in a couple of ways. Our chapters are encouraged to actively support local non-profits/charities through service projects and financial support. We take this a step further and donate a membership in each chapter to a non-profit or charity organization. These membership spots have all the benefits of normal chapter membership and allow the charity or non-profit the ability to network effectively and spread the mission of their organization. Ultimately, the non-profits benefit from added exposure and promotion by their chapter, as well as added educational benefit to the staff to go out and promote their non-profit to the rest of the community.

Our history of community involvement has allowed us to be associated with many local, national, and even international charities. As we grow, we want to continue to grow our community involvement as well. If you know a non-profit or charity that would benefit from being connected to a TEAM Referral Network chapter, please contact us!

From helping to stuff backpacks with school supplies, stocking food pantries, and attending galas, casino nights, golf tournaments and bowl-a-thons, to doing at-cost or in-kind donations, serving on committees, volunteering or sitting on boards, being mentors, building homes for Habitat for Humanity, or simply writing a check… TEAM members have impacted our non-profit TEAM members for over 15 years and will continue to do this "giving back" for many years to come.

Kelli Holmes, founder of TEAM Referral Network, has worked with thousands of businesses for over 25 years, specializing in teaching professionals how to GROW their business through relationships and referrals.

Today, TEAM has opened hundreds of chapters throughout the Western United States. It is a California-based franchisor company selling TEAM franchises with plans to expand further nationally and internationally.

TEAM provides a well-supported, structured, networking system, along with the networking tools, education and information needed for our members to grow their businesses.

My Mission to Patch the Planet
By Mitzi Ambrosio

What lies on the other side of pain?
What do you want it to be?
How badly do you want to get your life back?
Are you looking to embrace a new normal or to keep
fighting to get the life you had?
Would you give up an old way of thinking in order to get a
second chance?

As I sat on the cold tile floor, making sense of what just
happened and praying that help would come before another
kick from my mental health patient landed on my body, I
knew my life had took yet another twist. Recently divorced,
it felt I was being stripped away from my new-found
freedom. Just 3 months after closing escrow on a two-story
house, I found myself living with my sister. I suddenly
could not afford the mortgage anymore and it had become
too hard to climb the stairs to get to the bedrooms. Almost
3 years later, I was declared permanently disabled due to
the neck and back injuries I sustained from the incident. I
was still suffering from pain night and day and now I also
had to deal with the side-effects from the medications that
were supposed to help relieve pain: migraine headaches,
hot flashes, dizziness, heartburn, and stomach ulcers, to
name but a few.

I was in desperate need of relief for the constant pain, and
my health was deteriorating. I felt I had aged 10 years.
Since I did not walk with a limp or lose an extremity, I
would always get comments like, "You do not look like
you're in pain," or "It must be nice not to have to wake up
at 4 am to work at the hospital anymore."

Have you ever seen a fish at the market laying on a bed of ice so fresh that they look like they're only taking a break from swimming? Yet we know too well the harsh reality for the fish.

It took everything to be able to get out of bed every single day, determined to keep taking care of my boys even better than before now that I was home. Looking back, I know they were the reason I found the strength to keep going.

Caught in the web of Worker's Comp red tape, pharmaceutical bureaucracy, and a custody battle for my boys, guilt, anxiety, and hopelessness set in. I was in and out of depression. I prayed and yet I simultaneously mourned for the life I had, as I was starting to believe I was going to live the rest of my life in pain. With a "permanently disabled" label, I was facing a very limited opportunity to be able to provide for myself and my family. Who will ever hire me in my condition? Then a friend turned me on to real estate. I took a weekend class and studied for three days straight on my own and passed the test, only to find out later that driving clients around to look at houses proved to cause a great amount of back and neck pain.
My financial future looked bleak.

My answer came in the form of patches. Yes, of all things, pain-relieving patches that claimed to be non-invasive, drug-free and with no side-effects. Too good to be true? I thought so, too. Of all my various pain inflicting itself on my body, I was challenged to get patched for sciatica. As my pain began to subside within a few minutes, I exclaimed: "Where have you been all this time?"
My sciatica permanently went away with that first application. That weekend, I went dancing, as all those times I was laid up, one of my regrets was that I never took

the time to learn how to dance. I also gathered my family at my sister's house to share with them about the miraculous patches. They thought it was unbelievable as well and continue to use the patches to this day.

I had the opportunity to meet David Schmidt, CEO and inventor of the LifeWave Patch Technology in December, three months after I first experienced the patches. I was able to thank him for his invention and for giving my children their mother back. I knew that a million thank you's would never be enough. After hearing him speak, I realized the best way to show my gratitude was to pay it forward. No one, especially mothers, should have to wait 3 years like I did. That glimmer of hope becomes dimmer and dimmer with every single day spent in pain. Anger, bitterness, and loneliness are thieves that are so adept at altering your perception that before you know it, a "me against the world" battle wages within you. The sooner they can get back to being a mother to their children, to their role as a wife, as a productive citizen to the community, and back on their jobs or as entrepreneurs earning their own income, the better the world will be for everyone.

The irony is that my nursing career may have been over, but my injury led me to continue my purpose to serve others. With every pain I relieve, I am inspired to do more. I am inspired to be more. I am motivated to invest in the highest form of personal development to allow me to make the biggest impact faster.

Part of the assignment is to look back on my younger life and share three lessons to my younger self. I would like to note that I am convinced these lessons surfaced only after having been through NLP with Pivot Point Advantage. The learnings and partnerships gained through the program have truly elevated my life and are my motivation to answer the call to "patch the planet."

Lesson #1: Love and forgive yourself.
One day, I began to notice the lack of color and pretty things in my immediate environment. I then realized I had somehow believed I could only have pretty things once I measured up to my mother's expectation of me; once I had stopped disappointing her; once I had made her happy. I had been settling, holding back, and engaging in self-sabotage unconsciously, thinking that I did not deserve success. This revelation led me to further realize that I never loved myself and furthermore, that before I could truly love myself, I needed to forgive myself first.

That day, I realized I was doing to my eldest son exactly what my mother was doing to me, and that realization was the best thing that ever happened to my relationship with my son. All those years of lovingly coaxing him to go back to school to get a degree, sending him signals of "You can do better," I had missed out on celebrating his true accomplishments. Thankfully, I am now seeing what a fine gentleman my son has grown up to be.

Lesson #2: Nurture your dreams.
Allow yourself to dream; it helps keep the journey less bumpy and keeps you from quitting. If we live in a world where anything is possible, doesn't this mean everything is possible? Dream and dream big dreams.

    That beautiful secluded home with a spectacular view where the family gathers regularly

    That energy and vigor of pure health and joy

    That amazing relationship that gives meaning to life

    That freedom to travel the world and to spend precious time with loved ones

    That gratefulness to be able to touch lives for the better

Yes, you can have it all!
Light the fire and keep it lit. Wake up every day doing something to get you closer to your dream. Lay your head on the pillow each night, knowing it will all come true.

Lesson #3: Get out of your own way.
The sooner you embrace this lesson, the faster you will reach your goals. Remember to keep yourself from carrying your mistakes. Instead, put each one under your feet and use them as steppingstones to rise above them.

In the middle of writing my story, it occurred to me that one of the reasons I found it difficult to write this is, up until recently, I was not aware of the true impact I have made with the lives I have touched. I am now allowing myself to be in awe with what I have been doing for almost 9 years now. I proudly embrace people who are trying to get out of pain, giving them their health back, giving their life meaning again. It is a big deal—a very big deal. I recently heard Oprah address graduates of USC: "Pick a problem, any problem. Do something about it, because for one person, that something could be everything."

There is a form of art in Japan called kintsugi. It is the mending of broken pieces of pottery or a ceramic vase by filling the cracks with gold. They believe that when something has suffered damaged and has a history, it becomes more beautiful.

I received my new beautiful purpose as a blessing in disguise. A journey that began when I was first "patched."
   still strong yet more compassionate
   still determined yet more flexible
   still proud yet more grateful
   still guarded yet working on surrendering

Mitzi is an advanced wellness specialist and offers Breakthrough Patch & Nutrition Technology providing a non-drug solution to improve quality of life and to provide dynamic anti-aging effects. Be PAIN-FREE, improve your health, change your life and help others...this is LifeWave!

My Life and Music
By Marcy Sudock

Coming from a family that owned its own business, I grew up observing my parents' triumphs and struggles. A family business means the family works together. My brother and I participated in the business from an early age: labeling cans, selling, attending meetings, writing, shoveling, running errands, working trade shows, listening to the arguments, the stories, and learning from the never-ending optimism that permeated our home, even during the incredibly lean years when spaghetti or scrambled eggs were mana from Heaven. Like it or not, destiny and heredity had plans that I would be an entrepreneur. My dad was the consummate wheeler-dealer. He was the salesman's salesman, while my mother was the steady force and diplomat that made it all work. We were taught how to sell, how to write, how to read, how to listen for meaning, how to interpret, how and when to be quiet, how to read body language, and how to "close the deal."

From the time I was three years old, I remember thinking I had an electrified core running through my body from head to toe. This "electricity" was my energy, and I knew that everything was possible. I also knew I was here to fulfill a purpose and to be of service. As early as kindergarten, I was inventing service clubs and, by the second grade, I had joined Girl Scouts, where I learned the true meaning of service to others. Volunteerism has always been a big part of my life.

Music was always playing in our home, along with the constant dreaming, scheming, and planning. I cannot remember a time in my life when I did not want to participate in music. Piano would have been my first choice, but a piano was not a financial possibility, so when violin lessons were offered in school, a neighbor gave me a violin, and the wheels of destiny moved forward.

I was a good student, serving on student council, honor society, and numerous clubs, along with performing in my school orchestras and outside honor orchestras. The "electricity" was always flowing. Putting myself through college, I worked in a variety of jobs: bank teller, survey taker, retail sales in clothing and jewelry stores, going door to door selling Avon and Amway products, and always freelancing as a musician. Working as a musician and going to college was not sufficient to succeed. The skills learned from working in these various sectors was a great addition to my education. In college, I wanted to major in everything! Music became my major and my passion.

Mark Sudock and I were married on August 14, 1977, my senior year in college. We met in middle school and became a couple in my senior year of college. My wedding gown served a dual purpose: a wedding gown and a recital debut gown. Little did we know that those dual purposes would continuously intersect.

Mark and I created four amazing children. They became my music. Family is and always will be my number one passion. Two of our four children had medical challenges that required a great deal of money beyond what insurance would cover. Circumstances dictated that I continue working. How truly blessed I was to be able to help my family by making music.

One day, fate took a hand, and I injured my back. I was laid-up for a few months, but the income needs remained present. Taking that gift of time on my back as an opportunity to grow, I started Beautiful You Image

124

Consulting. Taking the skills honed in college and from the various jobs along the way, I produced a grand fashion show/women's empowerment luncheon in a major hotel to launch the new business. It was successful. I quickly became the "go to" gal for businesswomen who needed to present themselves in the business world. As a public guest speaker for numerous businesses and conferences, I helped women rise up and learn to be taken seriously, and I taught them to present themselves in a professional manner. It was a turning point in my career as an entrepreneur and as a woman of worth. When my back was completely healed, I gave up Beautiful You, and music, once again, became my income source, but this time with a twist.

Every setback is an opportunity for growth. It's committing to learning and moving forward that makes the difference. Beautiful You taught me how to network, how to build a business from the ground up, how to present, how to contract. The new business was launched: Heritage Chamber Ensembles and Strolling Strings, which morphed into Brocade International, Inc. with beautiful offices in Newport Beach's trendy Fashion Island. Brocade International, Inc. was a combination of high-quality live music performance and contracting, classical to jazz, recording, booking, and the first real 3-D mall on the internet, The Weddings and Celebrations Mall. The business thrived. We produced our first CD for weddings. I wrote the book *My Wedding Music Planner*. We performed thousands of weddings and parties for celebrities, politicians, and brides along with concerts. Brocade International/Heritage Chamber Ensembles and Strolling Strings were the ones to call. If it was a high-profile event, we were there. Then the unthinkable happened.

Just when everything was going great, we took our four children bowling. I was not going to bowl and risk my hands. Hence, I was not wearing the prescribed bowling "clown" shoes. The mommy in me went out to the lanes to help our four-year-old daughter. No bowling shoes, a well-intentioned mom and a well-oiled lane do not make for a good combination. With the grace of a bull in a china shop, I did a 360 onto the bowling lane, fracturing my left wrist into many small pieces. In one misstep, it appeared that a brilliant career would become a memory. We rushed to the hospital, where they told me of my shattered wrist and, in my mind at the time, they spoke of my shattered dreams. The next day, I was in surgery, where they pieced my wrist back together with three rods protruding from my wrist. Sense of humor still somewhat intact, I would joke that, if all else failed, they could slap a chicken onto the wrist rods and us me as a rotisserie. After a few weeks of self-pity, it was time to put on my big girl pants and make a plan. Not making music was akin to not being able to breathe. Those of you reading this who have a passion know what I am talking about. I made the decision that I was going to recover completely and be better than I was before. To that end, I went to physical therapy for my hand and wrist 5 days a week until insurance stated "no more." To help create this new reality, I sold my business to a trusted competitor. I also sold our online presence name, Brocade, to a well-known computer company of the same name. This took over the short fall when insurance would no longer contribute to physical therapy. I created my own therapy to rotate my left hand into the 80-90-degree turn required to play the violin, using therabands and the door as a fulcrum to work that hand around. It was a painful process that took nearly two years. I practiced bowing with my "good" hand every day, determined to have a great bow arm. After two years of making it happen, it happened! I was back to playing the violin. We've all heard the phrase "out of sight, out of mind." In the music business, you can't appear incapable or you are stricken from the list of those to call for work. It was time to start all over again. . .

Taking my retraining to heart, I went into privately teaching the violin. Who better could understand the foibles of learning to play the instrument than one who was at the top of her field and then needed to retrain her body to perform? I discovered that I loved teaching and was very good at it. I still teach and love helping my students discover the joy of music and the satisfaction that comes from accomplishment. I took on the job as group instructor for a local youth center, where I eventually became their music director, supplying and training teachers and presenting to six elementary schools and eventually expanding the program from 50 children to over 300 annually. This program became the feeder for the local middle schools and high schools in the area, helping them to thrive as well.

It's amazing how one phone call can change your life.

Early one morning, in 2000, I received a call from a colleague asking if I had a children's orchestra that might be interested in going on a concert tour of France. I said I would have one by that evening. After numerous calls to friends, colleagues, and students, we gathered that evening in my backyard, and Musique Sur La Mer Youth Symphony Orchestra was born. All the young musicians were just a bit over the beginner level of performance, and we only had eight weeks until we were off on our own tour d'France. The one-week tour was fast-paced, exhausting, and blessedly not well-attended by audience members. However, we had a great time, and this little ensemble became something very special, and I became not only a violinist, instructor, contractor and artistic director, but a conductor. For our first twelve years, we kept Musique Sur La Mer under the umbrella of the local youth center, retaining our autonomy but having the infrastructure of the youth center to enable our growth. During that time, the orchestra grew from one orchestra to five orchestras, as well as a variety of chamber ensembles: Musique Sur La Mer Youth Symphony Orchestra, Honors Chamber Orchestra, Honors Jazz Orchestra, La Petite Musique and the professional Musique Sur La Mer Orchestra. After those initial twelve years, the youth center decided our program was growing quite large, and it was time for us to leave the nest and fly, as our own non-profit had come. It was time. We became our own non-profit 501 c (3), and we soared, adding an orchestra day camp, expanded programs, a voice for new composers, and building relationships throughout Southern California and the world.

As of the publication of this book, we have performed numerous concerts within the United States plus concerts abroad in Australia (Sydney Opera House, Broughton College, Pittwater, Brisbane), New Zealand (Christchurch Cathedral, Hastings, Auckland, Wellington), Austria (Vienna's Musikverien-Saal, Salzburg Cathedral, Mozarteum, Mirabell Gardens, University of Salzburg, and the Esterhazy Palace in Eisenstadt), Czech Republic (Prague and Podebrady), Costa Rica (Teatro Nacional in San Jose, plus Arenal), France (Paris, Cannes, Nice), Wales, and England (as the American tribute to HH Prince William and Catherine Middleton in honor of their wedding, the Diamond Jubilee of HRH Queen Elizabeth II, the Royal College of Music, Hampton Court Palace, Blenheim Palace, Canary Wharf Music Festival.)

During our second tour to Australia to perform in the Sydney Opera House, I had a very minor heart attack while on the plane as it was descending into Auckland, New Zealand, where we were to change planes. I was rushed to the hospital by ambulance where they stopped my heart, restarted it, and I was relegated to remain in the ICU for three days. The "heart" incident was the result of a minor electrical problem in the heart that was later rectified in the US with an ablation. However, the newspapers turned it into a very big deal that had the potential of derailing a hard-earned career. As luck would have it, Bayer Aspirin was doing a national talent search for a spokesperson to star in a national healthy heart campaign. I took the audition, won the audition, and was the star of their commercial for five years plus full-page ads in national magazines, including *Woman's Day*. Once again, lemonade out of lemons, a healthy heart and numerous people helped through the campaign.

Our mission to empower musicians and create great music has enabled us to help numerous people with our music, locally and abroad. Thousands of children, teens, and adults have benefitted from our program. Our students have received partial and full scholarships to the world's most prestigious universities. They have become the musicians, doctors, teachers, lawyers, entrepreneurs, social workers, and parents who will shape our future. Our motto, "Music is the path, Musique Sur La Mer is the vehicle," holds true to this day.

We have raised awareness and funds for cancer patients, schools for the hearing impaired, food and coats for the homeless, funds to help sea mammals, Red Cross disaster relief, concerts for people in nursing homes, rehabilitation centers, senior centers and schools, served to help with beach clean-up, delivered holiday cards to veterans in the Veterans' Hospital in Long Beach, CA, sent thank you letters to soldiers, raised funds for the local children's hospital, and continue to use music to benefit humanity. We have partnered with the Long Beach Miller Children's Hospital supplying music for infirm children and their families. We have partnered with the Long Beach Aquarium of the Pacific, creating concerts that uplift and support ocean, waterways, and oceanic wildlife.

Every bit of this success is because passion and determination were the overriding factors when adversity would rear its head. In the course of this journey, I became a certified life coach and public speaker. My specialty is finding inner strength, raising humane and artistic children to become responsible, purposeful adults. My journey is not over. What comes next will unfold as the years expand. The richness of my life can be counted in the relationships made along the way and the mindful awareness achieved.

The core of "electricity" that I knew existed from the time of early childhood has waned on occasion, but the flicker has never gone out. Life will present itself in its best and worst forms. It is not a matter what life brings; it is a matter of how you choose to perceive it and what you do with it. Taking each situation as an opportunity for growth does not diminish sadness or place one in a state of denial; it empowers one to continue to have a joyous spirit and move forward, not despite adversity, but because of it.

For more information about Marcy Sudock and Musique Sur La Mer Orchestras and to become a supporting member of this worthy non-profit, go to our website: www.mslmorchestra.com.

Discovering Where Impact Really Resides:
A Journey Looking into Others' Eyes
By Rich Kozak, Founder/CEO of RichBrands

Rich's personal journey to making an impact in his own life, and in the lives of others, by looking into another's eyes and connecting, listening to their heart, seeing their vision and possibilities, then guiding them as they effectively step into their purpose.

"Phases Through Which Communication Evolves" read the infographic on the screen as the high-powered speaker consultant explained. "Performance, Presentation, Conversation and Connectedness." In a mere moment, it became clear to me: I have been evolving through those phases since childhood, and I see exactly where I am right now!

That moment, with its bright flash of clarity and perspective, made a permanent home in my conscious mind and enabled me to reflect on how my life experience has guided my evolution to impact, without my even knowing it.

My flash of clarity occurred ten years ago, in what I now refer to as "the love fest at the French hotel," sitting in a group of nineteen individuals. We had chosen to put ourselves into the hands of the famous speaker consultant, like clay on a potter's wheel, for our mentor to re-shape our rough edges and take away flaws that he and his team of heart-centered intuitive-types could sense so much more skillfully than we ourselves could. That bright flash kept re-appearing in my mind.

At that French hotel, everyone's intense energy was focused on helping each other quit playing small and step into greatness, and on leveraging the power of the spoken word masterfully delivered by one human being to impact an audience of many. Over our three-day process together, as we watched each other's clay being shaped, and as we heard the variety of world-changing work we each did, we developed a collegiality that prompted me to make the following offer.

"You all know that after seventeen years, I resigned my addictive career as the executive VP of a high-tech ad agency, and I don't do branding anymore. However, to honor each of you and what we have done here together, and to reinforce how powerful we can all be for each other, if any of you ever have a need in the area of defining your "desired brand," I want you to call me, and I will help you make your impact." My offer was genuine, but I considered the probability of any of them calling me to be remote.

That assumption was wrong because I had made an impact.

I am sitting here writing to you as a deeply experienced branding consultant. What's a branding consultant? A unique type of person who listens for the visions and desires of individuals who want to take their business and themselves to higher levels of significant impact on those whose lives they will touch. For me, the conscious thought, "Do I understand the impact I am making on this person?" began to surface only after years of well-intended attention-grabbing, which I learned is one of the prerequisite skills of making an impact.

I started my "performance" stage at an early age. I wanted to impress people with performance, but that wasn't a real impact. That was entertainment. In my youth, I was a strong student (lots of studying and good test-taking), and I had created two profitable businesses long before most of my peers had even thought about college. At thirteen, I began painting houses, and in high school, I continued my entrepreneurial activities by booking bands at fraternities. I learned to speak confidently from personal experience and to make it relevant to my listeners.

When I first started, I was doing "performance" in theater, playing in orchestras and singing in a rock band. I came to realize it was my enthusiasm and passion that attracted people to me. I also learned that being present with somebody else is where impact starts. It's about sitting nose to nose, shutting up and connecting with their heart, their passion. The more I realized I wasn't really impacting when I was performing, it became clear to me that the other phase of communication, "conversation," begins when you're present and connected.

Decades later, I received the blessing to become a communicator skilled in neuro-linguistics programming. I'm a trainer. I'm a shiny mirror, and I say, "Let me show you what I see in you. You're a mom, dancer, coach, whatever, and we're going to create a brand congruent with all those pieces of you."

Fortune 50: Personal Congruity

Before the ad agency, I spent years in industrial sales and marketing for a Fortune 50 company, which allowed me to learn a lot more about being personally congruent with what the brand stood for. If the brand stood for trustworthiness and integrity, I would be most congruent with the brand if I always did what I said I would do and always honored agreements. Making the brand's key characteristics come alive in my behavior that's congruent. The impact of the congruent behavior is to reinforce the brand identity of that employer on the mind of my customers. I learned how to make sure I was always doing that.

During my time at the Fortune 50 company, I volunteered in the leadership, serving as president of the American Marketing Association in Southern California.

It wasn't long until our cadre of volunteer leaders propelled the American Marketing Association's Southern

California Chapter to a special award. It became clear early in the explosion of volunteerism that my passion, energy, positive forward motion, and uplifting language were the most effective tools I had in order to impact other potential volunteers, encouraging them to take part. Honest, authentic encouragement worked like rocket fuel for volunteers who had lots of other choices about how to spend their free time in Southern California. Those characteristics led to the success of the impact that the professional association had during the years of my involvement. I've watched that impact on volunteers who were inspired, as they became passionate about what they were creating.

One impact of our recognition for outstanding programming in Southern California was my election as vice president of business marketing to the Board of Directors of the American Marketing Association International.

At the Agency it had taken me 33 years to get my "presentation" and "performance" behaviors into my "comfort zone" before beginning my 17-year run at the agency. The phases of communications I used to engage and move audiences as an agency executive were mostly "professional presentation," a must in the boardroom, occasionally punctuated by "professional performance." In the high-stakes world of ad agencies courting billion-dollar companies, it's a prerequisite to earn their trust and to ensure that they believe in your alleged passion for their business. As business-to-business marketing consultants, the agency had to build solid credibility with facts and logic before emotional engagement could become part of the process. Showing decision makers my genuine passion for their world engaged the emotions that built personal chemistry and created a mystique for the agency. Sounds logical, yes?

Through those years of building relationships, I would learn that "Conversation" is the stage of communication where impact really begins, and

"Connectedness" with the heart of another is the foundational place where one can see another's possibilities, in some cases more clearly than they can themselves. I now ask a business, "Tell me, when your brand thrives, what are the highest-level impacts you can envision yourself making on the world you touch? You have a heart for something. What is it?"

We write the impacts clearly, then we run towards impact.

During my agency years, it had not yet been revealed to me that within the next two decades I would be empowering businesspeople to guide the impacts they envision making on the individuals and the worlds they will touch.

When I was with the agency, I was attracted by the opportunity to help each client company evolve by reshaping its brand, identity, and reputation. The real impact I was after was establishing belief in the agency's mystique and its power to guide the client through its branding process. In my years as an agency exec, I didn't know then that today I would be helping entrepreneurs to guide the impacts that they wanted to make on the world.

You can't just go in there and talk at a client. You have to listen. You learn to be extremely present and shut up. Through years and years, I finally got good at it.

For example, I met with a lawyer who serves as a consultant to criminal defense attorneys to protect immigrant clients and guide their pleadings. I talked to her about her personal history, background, and thoughts. I listened deeply and copied exactly what she said, because I needed to get into her "zone" to understand the impacts she envisions. I do a heart-connect with people. All my experience has designed me to do that. I didn't know that during those seven years at Alcoa. I didn't know it when I got elected to the international board of the American Marketing Association.

This whole dance, from the early audiences of my Performance and Presentation to my Conversation and Connectedness with my branding clients today, has evolved around impact. I've come back to branding after 12 years. Now, I'm using this ability that has evolved over all these years to hear and see and feel what impact businesses and individuals make when they thrive. I help them write that down from their heart.

Today, I help individuals who will someday have big businesses to make an impact on the groups of people they want to touch.

Every impact is a pebble tossed in the water whose ripples are more far-reaching than I ever imagined.

It's been a long journey, and I feel like I'm just getting started; it's as though I'm finally fulfilling my purpose: helping other people find their purpose. It feels like love instead of work, and I feel like I'm twenty-five, because my first book, *The Brand YOU Will Become: How to Define It and the Steps to Achieve It,* is only the first in a series of books. One will lift up God's glory. God is good. I'm proud I have this gift. I'm lucky. I feel like the luckiest man in the world.

Today, I live where "conversation" meets "connectedness." I live it and I teach it. I left the agency after seventeen years. Twelve years later, I quit saying, "I don't do branding anymore." Now I realize I'm supposed to be doing this because God put this gift in my heart, and I'm supposed to use it. Why did I write this book? Because impact is a process you can learn. You can guide a fourteen-billion0dollar company or a single teenager with this process. You can use it for your business and your children. Once you understand the process, you don't need me. Now you can change your life and impact your kids. You can be a leader at your church, your professional association, or Kiwanis.

If we always start with impact, it will change people's behavior towards one another. We're going to touch a lot of lives here! Get a grip, take a breath, read the book, come to the workshop. Get on with it. Leave the planet having made an impact.

That is my significance and my legacy.

Rich Kozak is the founder of RichBrands.
He effectively serves any business or individual professional who is determined and committed to grow faster, to become known as outstanding, and to make significant impacts on people's lives and on the world. You accelerate your impact when you define The Brand YOU Will Become.

Awareness is Pure Magic
By Monica Weber Shoukair

Have you ever found yourself feeling scared, unloved, alone and lost? It can be very frightening. That is exactly how I felt in my young age. I didn't understand why I hurt or why I felt so alone. Life forced me to switch into survival mode early in life, numbing my brain and voiding my voice from the fear of more hurt.

I could share sorrows from my childhood, but instead, I choose to let go of the stories. I chose to move forward as these exact frightening and sometimes unpleasant stories are the exact ones that made me the strong woman I am today. I am now in charge of how I remember those unpleasant and perhaps traumatic moments.

It is up to me to choose what to do with my past. Today, I have decided to re-write those stories so they serve me in a positive way. The choice is mine. Being a victim is far from what serves me, and being stuck in the past attracts negativity into my life. I elect to embrace and accept the wisdom that these challenging moments gifted me.

Today, I'm empowered as a result from the hurt, the anger, the fear and all the emotions that I experienced in the past. Letting go has been incredibly wonderful. I'm aware there are times in which I still fall, I still make mistakes and my journey continues to have bumps and moments of rough terrain. I can agree that now when I fall, I am only left with letting go, finding solutions and getting back up again, because this is what serves me best: the conviction of getting back on track and the determination of understanding that this time around, I can reach higher, be stronger and better. I have been blessed to have been exposed to uncomfortable experiences that gave me the opportunity of stretching my being. It is through these experiences that I stretch and grow. I now can accept that it all was a master plan to develop and polish who I have become.

Have you ever felt as if you were a survivor? Then together we can say, we survived! We are here at this precise moment to conquer all that we get to create every day. What we do with the time we are given on this earth and with the time we have left to live is up to us. Without these experiences, I am certain that today my life would be very different, and not necessarily in a positive way.
Every little thing has an energy, everything moves, and life evolves daily. I develop myself daily, and as I look at this incredible life through the right colored glasses, it showers me with constant gifts that stretch me. Little by little, these gifts push me to a higher and higher level of consciousness. Magically, when I am ready for more learnings, the right teacher seems to find me, and the learnings appear.

Forgiveness has been a big part of growth, and I have learned that forgiveness is for the victim more than for the offender. I opened my heart to learn what forgiveness was all about, and it has empowered my life in many ways. As I empower myself, I am able to empower others. Also, through this process, I have had the gift of finding my voice and being more open. Throughout it all, I have had the opportunity to help others.

There is a warrior inside me, and it is me who gets to do what I want. It was an incredible feeling to shed the weight I was carrying on my shoulders from the learnings that did not serve me. I got rid of the backpack that I was carrying on my back, filled of guilt and negative thoughts. I had been like a turtle that constantly carried their heavy shell everywhere they went without a choice.

140

My journey brought me the opportunity to raise three amazing kids, now young adults. Today, they are independent and successful. I am a holistic health practitioner, and throughout my studies, I have been able to assist people healing themselves for the past 17 years.

I also owned a botanical skin and hair care business for 3 years. Although this business ended up not delivering the results I expected to receive, there were many unbelievable learnings in the experience through the process. Sometimes, we must lose big to see what we have refused to pay attention to.

What is next? Life! A life full of freedom and opportunities to create vibrant moments and exciting memories. I get to love myself. I get to value, accept and respect myself. The magic is in having the wisdom to comprehend that only when I am in a great place with myself am I ready to overflow and share my blessings and gifts with others.

Have you ever experienced failing over and over due to not being still long enough so one can listen to what the inner voice desperately wants to whisper? Cleaning my world from all the noise and from all that was confusing me was a necessary step to move forward. When I got myself to be still, when I trusted, and when I felt grounded was when I finally was able to identify my inner wisdom shining at its best, and only then is when things began to simply work beautifully and magically.

Life taught me the importance of loving myself and to be a priority to me before anything else. I have learned that I must value who I am, accept and respect myself lots and lots before I can truly value, love, accept and respect someone else. I keep working daily to practice and practice, and I continue daily to change old habits.

Blaming my past for my current misery is technically blaming myself for having created the things that don't serve me, for sabotaging myself day in and day out. I am aware now that it is up to me to take responsibility in living life with the awareness that I am the one who creates every step of what takes me to what I desire, in valuing life enough to know that I'm responsible to live with impeccability.

What would happen in your life if you began today, with all your passion, to love who you are, to respect yourself and to live life without allowing yourself to be one hundred percent excuse-less?

Today, I know that positive thinking spills into positive actions, and from those positive actions, daily miracles happen. I also realize that listening is imperative and that at any given time before I speak or act, it is best to think and pause so I can choose my words intelligently and appropriately. Instead of saying more, often it is best to say less. At times, it was challenging to think positively, to think and then say to myself what would serve me better than shouting a four-letter word that would be accompanied by a long list of other words that are omitted in all spelling bee competitions. And those words would always come handy when I was feeling defensive, frustrated, angry, fearful and all the emotions that I experienced when I felt insecure, scared, ungrounded and sagacious.

Now, I am aware that when I lose my temper and I react to others, I am reacting to myself. When I criticize, I am criticizing myself. When I have anger towards someone, I have anger towards myself. When I say something unpleasant, I'm talking to myself, and the list continues like this with every negative emotion that can exist within me, within us.

Propelling myself to a higher place has required changing many old habits. Old habits are deeply engraved inside us in our subconscious, yet with a strong mind set, shift is possible. We can shift these old habits to entertain new and exciting ones. I have learned best through moments of adversity.

The learnings have cultivated wisdom; they have transformed spirituality and physical strength within me. They have also helped me make a difference in my life through my work, one person at the time.

Awareness is pure magic. I tell myself daily to love more and to invest more, following my heart and being more aware of my inner voice. I trust myself, as the right answers always reside within me, and I remind myself that fear is dark and to let go of doubt.

One day at a time, one shift at a time, one idea at a time, one concept at a time, one deep breath at a time, one minute of exercise at a time, shedding one pound at a time. It is about that one little change we do daily on a consistent basis that will bring the results we desire. One of anything on a consistent basis is what creates a new habit. Habits make a difference and create the necessary shifts that then create the life we want and deserve.

Dream and dream and dream some more. Want it passionately and never give up!

I want to continue cultivating the ability to re-set, re-align, re-start, re-claim, and re-ignite to make a difference among humanity. I invite you to join me today in a journey filled with love, respect and impeccability towards ourselves.

Monica is a holistic health practitioner (HHP) in Eastern and Western therapies, and she has provided her services throughout a private practice for the last 17 years. Monica holds a national certification for her HHP studies and is always eager to learn more; she continues to educate through extracurricular courses. Making a difference one person at a time is her goal and passion. Spending time with family, traveling and the outdoors are some of her favorite things.

What a Mind Can Conceive, It Can Achieve
By Dale Fukuda

My name is Dale Fukuda, a baby boomer born at the Dee
General Hospital, February 23, 1946,
In Ogden, Utah.

During my early years growing up in Ogden, I was
protected from some feelings toward Japanese that my
parents and relatives encountered. I was always encouraged
to "fit in" and "get along" with everyone. My parents never
talked about the treatment of the Japanese or internment
camps. I learned that on my own later. During that time
growing up, family was very important. I was the oldest of
all of 10 cousins, a brother and sister. Being the oldest, I set
the example of proper behavior and ethics. I was still able
to have a fun childhood. I think helping relatives grow up
gave me a sense of pride in being able to help with positive
influence.

When I was 8 years old, my parents moved to Los Angeles,
giving my brother, sister and myself a chance to be exposed
to a multicultural environment with opportunities for more
growth and education. I was fortunate that during
elementary school, junior high and high school, I had a
variety of friends from all different backgrounds, including
food choices, ideals, spiritualities and thought processes. It
was at that time that I became a student of people and
started forming the values of what is right or wrong. I was
able to "fit" in with the gangs without becoming a gang
member. I fit in with the hi-water surfers, bloods and
Buddhaheads. During that time, none of those terms were
derogatory. As time and attitudes changed, I learned how to
adapt and become politically correct. I saw people who
obtained money and material things illegally and those who

earned it ethically. I decided at 16 years old that I was going to own a "legit" business.

At age 15, while going to high school, my after-school baseball career shifted to working part-time in a grocery school. The small neighborhood grocery store experience added more responsibilities that I embraced. I guess my work ethics and willingness to learn everything in the grocery business made the owner and manager comfortable as they gave me more responsibilities every week. During the summer, I was able to set my full-time work schedule while filling in with the cashier and butcher to give them a lunch break. All weekly ordering, cleaning, shelf stocking, and unloading of the truck that made deliveries was up to me to schedule and "get it done." In those days, 50 cents an hour was the starting rate, so I felt accomplished and appreciated that by the end of the summer, I was making $1.75/hr. I bought my first car and was able to afford the maintenance and insurance.

Ahhh...I was 16 years old, independent, and moving forward. Those were fun times building relationships, looking forward to graduating and going on to college. Service clubs, giving back to the community, the Baldwin Dam breaking, helping others, working—all these things during high school were preparing me for more.
When it was time to "buckle down" for college, I decided to go to Cal State Los Angeles instead of U.C.L.A. to stay away from friends who were going to attend. I met new people and got into a good study habit that had escaped me in my senior year of high school.
S.I. Hayakawa (language in thought and action) had a large impact on me, as I learned, it's not the words that are important, but how you leave a person feeling.
I moved on to working full-time in a photo lab to support my flair for fast cars, my eating habits and my part-time, 2-

year college stint. I guess working 10 hours a day, partying into the late night and playing cards instead of going to class didn't help my GPA, so I dropped out of college and worked full-time up to 12 hours a day.

It's interesting as I look back now the impact that a high school teacher made when she said that Japanese are good at copying things and not good at leadership or building a business.

At that point, I decided to prove the old teacher's comment wasn't going to dictate my future.

Working full-time in a photo lab, in addition to developing film, making color prints and all the photographic services (some of which no longer exist), I became a color photo analyst, which connected me to the top photographers and advertising agencies in the Los Angeles area.

I practiced how I made people feel when I visited ad agencies and worked with photographers as an outside sales/customer service person who made suggestions on what type of prints to make and on any color corrections and changes that were needed. All preparation for photo editing was done with the old hand techniques before Photoshop. This new process of getting out into the public made me draw on my previous experiences to get comfortable driving to a client's location and bring value to the client. Little did I know then, I was building relationships that made clients comfortable with my knowledge as they introduced me to other companies. In those days, art directors belonged to groups of other art directors who worked for ad companies and big businesses that had their own art and marketing department. These client relationships became a referral group that introduced me to other people looking for my expertise. These introductions brought me to other ad agencies—top companies like Carnation, and other industries like printing, auto, and publishing to name a few. One of the referrals was to a large printing and reproduction company that was putting in a scanner to make color separations. This new technique in creating lithographic film to make plates for printing presses would eventually replace the old hand techniques. The requirement to scan an image was to shoot a transparency (type of film). Any large original print or painting could not be wrapped around the scanning drum. That's where I came in to use a specialized large camera to shoot a picture on a 4" x 5" transparency film that could be used to scan. The nature of what the scanner interpreted as to what to produce in a 4-color lithographic piece of film was not accurate. There were neutral areas that created the separations of color for making plates that came out red. To compensate for the scanner's interpretation, I had to create a formula that when shooting the transparency of the camera, the photo looked green. My name and reputation led me to working part-time in a lithographic film color separation business, where I combined photographic techniques with newfound lithographic techniques making film to be used to make printing plates. I continued weekends when I got married. It was my first marriage, with a new house and a move to Orange County. I applied as a "cameraman" for a job in a printing company that made its own separations by hand. They hired someone and needed a salesperson. After 18 months, becoming the top salesperson with accounts like a book publisher, a magazine publisher that I sold primarily the "film work" to led me to 6 of the top business that I did printing for.

The person who hired me at my "part-time job," and who gave me an opportunity to segue into a whole new world, was going to start his own business with another person. The 3-person corporation was formed. One person was responsible for the financial portion of the business, and another person was responsible for the manufacturing of the product. I was to bring in business.

The relationships I had developed started to pay off with securing business from a variety of advertising agencies, printers and other businesses. The biggest account I got was Capitol Records. A lesson learned: find a way to develop multiple businesses for income stream. Capitol Records become 50% of the revenue. Capitol Records payed invoices at exactly 60 days. The finance person would not work within the Capitol system of approvals for payments and demanded invoices to be paid in 30 days or an interest rate would be added to the invoice for late payments. After the meeting with Capitol Records stating that if I ever left, they would take all their business elsewhere, as they would never work with Chromagraphics again.

Within a month, I left Chromagraphics, with an understanding that the non-compete clause would be waived in lieu of any money from the sale of the stocks. Ironically, a person that I met when I started with Chromagraphics, started his own business about the same time. He was a one-man band with one account that was publishing pornographic material. We came to an agreement of a 50/50 partnership, in Wilmington, CA. Six months later, the old account was replaced with the solid reputable business that followed me. Many late hours, many road miles and our first year finished with $800.00. Time to hire people. My sister-in-law helped part-time while she went to college. Orbis Graphic Arts, Inc. moved to Orange County.

I went to school learning motivation, sales managing, and accounts receivable/payables. I made mistakes and kept growing. We bought our own building, put in the second Chromacom system in the United States. The system required building a "clean room" like in the aerospace industry. The system was a complete retouching, image assembly that would change the printing industry. Laptops and computers today have more power and memory than the old $250,000 system. Yes, then there was the cost of the scanner. As the industry started to get more technologically advanced, adding a printing press was the next step. Buying the third Akiyama press made in Japan required a trip abroad. This new press would compete with the industry leaders at a more affordable price. After 18 years of marriage and 15 years in business, the workaholic lifestyle that had built an 8-million-dollar printing business took its toll on my family life. The song "Cat in the Cradle" had me break down and cry, as I worked to find a balance with my wife and family, but it was too little too late. Paying for a wife to go on trips without me was not ideal. So, we did the California split of assets. The children went to the wife and the debts went to me. I had to start over.

After a few years and some high-paying corporate managing positions, I decided that corporate politics was not what I wanted, so I worked as a salesperson for different companies during my second marriage. A house in Corona and a beautiful daughter, and the decision to have my graphic design wife go full-time as a business, kept me married trying to do the "right thing." I was the sales end of her business and I set up printer relationships for her to offer a complete design/printing service. That relationship led me to TEAM Referral Network as I started as an in-home wine-tasting consultant.
I really got into the networking idea and leveraged my membership by following all the recommendations.
I've had to rebrand myself and start over multiple times, and with the help of Stacey O'Byrne and NLP, I have been able to learn many important lessons that help give me a strong purpose in life. David Schmidt and LifeWave have

brought a new health technology that enables me to help people live a longer, healthier live.

The sharing of my experiences using the tools of communication to those I meet have started to impact their health and financial life.

Moving forward, my wish is for each person to be honest with themselves, to find their love and purpose in life and to help touch lives in a positive manner. Know that whatever a mind can conceive, it can achieve.

If each person would help a person's life shift to the better, and if this chain reaction continued, it would make for an exciting world.

Training Wheels
By Dr. Candace Davis

One of the biggest impacts on my life has been my
relationship with my daughter. There have been many
learning experiences gained from our relationship that have
had a profound impact on my life. Let's begin with my
most memorable Christmas with her.

It was Christmas Eve, and I was preparing dinner for our
annual Christmas Day party. Keith, my husband, an E.R.
physician, had left for work and my six-year-old daughter,
Micaela, was in the kitchen getting the milk and cookies
together in anticipation for Santa's after midnight visit. I
asked, "Are you sure you don't want anything for
Christmas this year?" She replied, "No Mom, nothing in
particular, but I don't mind being surprised with
something." I thought this was oddly unlike my child, but I
went with it. "Okay, you've been good, so I'm sure Santa
will come up with something special for you." It was way
past her bedtime, so I let her know it was okay to leave the
milk and cookies on the stool next to the fireplace and
prepare for bed. She did just that: left the snack for Santa,
got ready for bed, said her prayers, and fell fast asleep.

As I returned to the kitchen, I thought about our
conversation before she put the snacks out for Santa.
Micaela asked me if Santa was real or make-believe. I told
her the spirit of Santa was real. She wasn't satisfied with
that answer, and frankly, I'm not sure what it meant. It
sounded like it was the right thing to say. She was only six
years old, and I wanted her to enjoy the fantasy, the fun,
and the excitement of Santa Claus. Kids seem to grow up
too fast these days.

"So, you mean there's not really a Santa?" she asked.

"I'm saying, if you believe in Santa, then he is real. Now,
get to bed."

I was desperately trying to end the conversation to escape these difficult questions. I wondered what the spirit of Santa meant to me. Am I simply feeding my daughter a white lie to prolong her childhood imagination and to prevent the ripping away of her innocence? Maybe.

Just then, I remembered I should put away the cookies and milk and put out a few gifts for her underneath the tree. As I lifted the saucer that held the cookies, I discovered a piece of folded paper with a message to Santa. With a little guilt, I read Micaela's private note.

> Dear Santa, my friends say you are not real. Mom and Dad think I don't want anything for Christmas, but I do. If you get me these things, then I know you are real. Here is my list: a red rose, sparkly make-up, earrings, a necklace, clothes, books, and a bicycle. Thank you and Merry Christmas!

There were seven items on Micaela's list, and Keith and I had only purchased one item: the bike. Our plan was to bring out the bicycle from the garage early on Christmas morning. I went into panic mode. I grabbed a pair of scissors, put on my jacket, opened the front door, and searched our dark garden for a rose. It was the one thing on her list I could find at such a late hour. After five minutes, I came across a perfect flower in the moonlight. One missing rose wouldn't hurt!

On Christmas morning, with other gifts for the family, there was a brand-new bicycle and a beautiful single red rose wrapped in pink ribbon underneath the tree. The rest of the day would just have to depend on her attitude.

It began like most Christmas mornings at our house: hectic, fun, and filled with love. There was much preparation for our expected guests. My daughter, husband, and I all dressed in festive African clothing of sapphire blue and gold-colored cloth. Teaching Micaela to embrace her

African heritage meant a lot to us, as parents, and this year, we looked spectacular!

When it was time to open presents, Micaela went straight for the bike. The rest of her gifts were opened quickly, wrappings thrown everywhere. The rose, however, was handled slowly with meticulous care and wonder. As she gently picked it up, she looked at me with a perplexed smile and whispered, "Mom?" She appeared to have lost her thought for a moment. I then offered to place her rose in a small vase atop the fireplace. She accepted my offer and happily cleaned up her mess, so she could go outside and practice riding her first "big girl" bicycle with no training wheels.

Training wheels (n.)- a supportive set of back wheels on a bike to assist new learners in balancing and riding by themselves.

It was in those next moments, while watching her ride her shining new bike without the training wheels, it all made sense. Her curiosity in Santa led me to a learning experience of my own. That morning and the night before served as preparation to let go of the training wheels. Our little girl was growing up. She was curious about life's mysteries, and she was trying to differentiate realism from myths and fairytales. All her life, she had been given training wheels to prevent her from falling into despair, disappointment, and injury. At that moment, I realized I could do nothing about the chatter she would be hearing from her friends, her older cousins, and television. Although it would be some time before she would no longer need our support, I knew it was important for Micaela to make up her own mind and explore the possibilities that the world would present to her. I would have to learn to respect her decisions and trust she would learn to ride without training wheels, even if that meant falling in the process at times and succeeding other times.

I asked myself how I should proceed with the rest of the day if she chose not to believe in Santa. After all, she did not receive most of the gifts on that list. Would this note ruin her Christmas and bring disappointment? Should I reveal to her I found the note?

No, I dropped the training wheels and let us all ride this out.

Micaela's grandmothers were the first guests to arrive, followed by her aunt, cousins, uncles, and their families. Many brought gifts for Micaela, even the girlfriend of one of her uncles whom we had never met. My friend Dawn brought glitter lipstick for little girls. One of her grandmothers brought her new earrings and a matching necklace; the other, a beautiful pink coat. She had cousins and uncles that brought her every book and toy she could long for. By the end of the day, after all the company had come and gone, Micaela realized she had received everything on her list and more.

It was a spectacular day. Very few things in life take me by complete surprise the way this Christmas did! I can't honestly remember a time when I believed in Santa as a child, but I do, however, believe in miracles.

That night before tucking her into bed, the question arose once again. "Is Santa real?" she asked me with sleepy eyes. This time, I knew just what to say.

"Christmas miracles are real, so I do believe the spirit of Santa is real, but only you can decide what is true in your heart and mind."

That was the Christmas my daughter got a single red rose and a bike without training wheels. It was also the day l relinquished control and learned to trust in this beautiful thing called life because, sometimes, it all works out the way it should.

At ChiroMed Healing Center, Dr. Davis focuses on an integrated approach, which includes patient history, lifestyle, X-rays, and a thorough physical, orthopedic, and neurological exam to help determine the best individualized treatment for you. Dr. Davis is knowledgeable, experienced, passionate, and spends as much time as needed with each patient.

Dr. Davis specializes in extremity adjustments, as well as spinal adjustments. She treats the shoulders, elbow, wrist, as well as the hip, knees, or pelvis. Dr. Davis also includes soft tissue mini massages, mobilization and stretching with adjustments.

My Multi-Dimensional World
By MaryLou Hunter, Ph.D

I grew up on eighty acres, and I was the middle child of five siblings. Mom had her hands full, and I had a ton of free time to roam and talk to the trees, rocks, animals, and well, just about anything in sight. I always knew that I was different, and if I ever thought for one moment I was normal, my siblings would always remind me of my unique personality. Their exact description of me was, "You are a fruit-loop." Although growing up, I was misunderstood and frankly, I sometimes confused myself as reality was always shifting. One minute I was playing with my dolls and the next I was in another world, visiting, mending and healing, yet I always had the ability to smile and continue moving forward and somewhat carefree. I have pondered this thought: I am carried through life protected by my own perception of me.

Being able to feel energies around me has made the most impact in my life as a child and as an adult.

I remember at three years old, we lived on a ranch that my dad worked. The house was an old ranch home that was home of many souls. I could feel different energies in each room. Not all the energies were nice. I remember hearing them at night when we were supposedly sleeping. I would hear walking on the floor and even see shadows dart across the room. I don't ever remember being afraid. Somehow, I knew that the white light around me was protecting me. I never told anyone what I saw and heard. I always stayed in my own little world. I knew that no matter what passed me by, I was ok and protected.

Growing up, there were times I would pick up objects, mostly rocks, and when I picked them up, I would feel different emotions and even temperatures and vibrations. I still have some of those rocks and I use them in my healing treatments. Each one has a different attribute and they tell me what to use them for. I knew this even as a child. I would like to sit by the trees and feel their heart beat and watch their branches dance with joy. My dad even built me a treehouse so that I could be closer to the nature of the trees. It was also a place to escape for hours and not get in trouble for daydreaming, aka being in another world. For the most part, I was more comfortable being alone, always wandering off, yet I was never alone.

When I was twenty-five, I was in my dad's study and a dark energy came from a carved stone that was sitting on his bookcase. I was reading and suddenly, it felt extremely cold in the room. My heart was beating so hard I thought I was having a heart attack. I looked up and saw a gray matter come out from the carved stone, which was across the room and flew right in front of my face. I did not fear this presence, even though it was trying to frighten me. I remember staring at it; it seemed like forever, but it was only a few seconds. I felt courage from deep within me and told it to get out of my face and the energy went away and the room became warm again.

I remember driving on the freeway with my daughter in the backseat. She was in her car seat and traffic was moderate. We were singing to a children's music CD when suddenly, I felt something grab my steering wheel and make a sharp left turn. I looked around at all the cars around me and I knew at that point, we were going to be in a serious car accident. I looked up to the sky and asked angels to protect me and I saw two lights come down from the sky to my car. I also saw a white wall of energy circle around me and then I saw everything in slow motion. I must have blacked out because the next thing I remember was looking up and all the cars around me stopped; no one was hit, and I backed up and drove back in my lane and started driving again. It was as if everything stopped and the world around me was completely still. I felt as if I was traveling in time as the angels were protecting me.

When I was in sales as a young adult, I would make cookies during the holidays and deliver them to my customers with their purchases. My customers were mostly elderly women, as I had made it one of my missions to spend extra time with them and they really enjoyed the company. It was a rainy day and I loaded up all their purchases and cookies into my Mazda RX7. I was ready and all my customers were excited and waiting upon my arrival. I turned the ignition on, and the car was completely dead. I guess I could have called roadside service to change out the battery, but that didn't even cross my mind. I tried a few more times to start the car and nothing happened. I just sat there for a couple of minutes, thinking this can't be happening! I must not let anything get in the way of visiting my customers. If anyone was watching me, they must have thought I was a crazy woman as I was talking to the energy of my car, explaining my desire to visit my customers. I remember sending healing energy to the battery and demanding in love that I needed to start the car and drive. I remember how I felt. I had no doubt that the car would start when I turned the ignition, and it did!

As a young adult, I started experiencing deep connections to random people in my life. I would see a person walk by and have a gut feeling that they needed something. I could feel their emotions and then get a deep desire to send them some sort of a blessing. At first, it was occasionally I would get the feeling but now it is continuous, and I am not even in their presence. They just pop up in my mind and I am always sending blessings and healings.

My dad had a cyst on the back of his neck. He left it alone for years; I watched it get bigger. He always complained about it, not that it hurt. It was annoying because it was visible, and he was self-conscious. One day out of the blue, he asked me to lay my hands on it. The next day, it was gone and never came back. What was interesting about this story is we never talked about my healing abilities, yet he knew he could channel his healing through me.

I had a client who came in with severe pain in her right leg. She said she had this pain for as long as she could remember, and it seemed to be getting worse. Originally, she hired me as her massage therapist. I told her before the massage that I was an energy healer and asked her permission to add energy healing to her massage. Of course, she said yes, not even knowing what that fully meant. I work with my spirit guides and sometimes I get pictures pop up in my head. This is one of the ways my guides talk to me. The number eight came up and when I asked her what happened to her at eight years old, she started crying and told me that was the year she was raped by her uncle. After doing some shamanic work on her, she got up off the massage table completely free of pain.

I have had thousands of experiences like the ones I just shared with you. Ever since I can remember, I could see, feel and know things that are relevant to our physical and spiritual world. I have always had the ability to travel in other realms. It's not unusual for me to sit peacefully and talk to the energy of a tree while interceding on someone's behalf in addition to traveling across the realms for various sorts of reasons from pleasure to spiritual warfare. If I knew growing up what I know now, I would have told myself as a child to embrace the gift. You are not a fruit loop; you are an energy healer.

My abilities to work with energy has given me so much clarity when it comes to healing. So many people are walking in a world of trance. They have lost their purpose and passion. They have unknowingly drowned in their sea of anger, sadness, fear, hurt and guilt. It is my passion and my purpose to bring back the light in their lives. By helping people shift their perceptions, they can shift their life and reach for the desires of their hearts.

Energy is always moving and has vibration. When you understand how to master the energy in your life, you make clear the path of abundance, whatever that means to you. It's a spiritual journey that is always teaching the lessons you want to learn that allows personal growth. Learning to move energy around you, both internal and external, can help clear stagnation in your life. My goal is to share what I know so that I can heal the world one person at a time.

Hi, I'm MaryLou Hunter, Ph.D.

I am extremely open and love what I do. I have an amazing family. I am a caring and loving wife and a mom of two amazing daughters. I am blessed to have a grandson who gives me joy in my life.

I am very metaphysical and am always doing healing work in several places, planes, all at the same time. I think my proudest moments as a mom is when my children come to me for hands-on healing instead of reaching for the medicine cabinet for over-the-counter drugs and when they ask me to feel their energy to make sure they are balanced. I have been helping clients improve the quality of their lives for 20 years. As an INTRA-personal communication expert, I specialize in helping people understand who they are, how they develop habits and gain insight in personal growth. I help you to understand and develop intuition with the energy around you and in your personal space. I feel my expertise in holistic life coaching along with my knowledge in energy and shamanic healing and nutrition offers a complete holistic coaching experience.

I have completed my doctorate in holistic life coaching. I have a holistic health degree among several certifications in nutrition, life coaching, aromatherapy, hypnotherapy and neuro-linguistic programming (NLP).
I am a shamanic Reiki master teacher and a shamanic counselor.
I studied psychology at California State University, Long Beach, and spiritual psychology at a local theological institute. I am an ordained minister and am a published author of the book *Soulful Freedom*.
I have created many techniques and have inspired students to live their life at their highest vibration. My goals are to educate the importance of life balance through intra-personal spiritual/self-development. My mission is to bring back the simplicity of health through natural means of nutrition and to heal the soul by focusing on the emotional toxicities and bringing back the parts of the soul that have been lost for various reasons. My passion in life is helping people get back to the first step to healing, which is to love yourself unconditionally.
Once you understand that, you will begin to live.

My Past Created Me
By Stacey O'Byrne

All my life, I wanted to make a difference. I wanted to
make an impact. I didn't know how or what, or even what
that meant. I just knew I wanted to, needed to make a
difference. I had what looked on the outside as a "blessed"
life. Some would have said I was born with a silver spoon
in my mouth. Reality was the complete opposite. I was
born into an upper middle-class family, so we were
comfortable financially. I will avoid going down the pain of
growing up with an alcoholic, over-achieving father whose
demands and expectations of me were—well, we'll call
them *character building*. I remember being so hungry for
his attention and his approval. He always seemed to give it
unconditionally to my younger brother for everything, yet
for me, no matter what I did, it was never good enough. I
believe it was that conditioning that put me on my pursuit
of excellence, because that is exactly what I felt I had to
strive for to get that elusive "good job." When my mother
lived with us, she did her best to balance it out; however,
half of a whole is still only half. When my mother divorced
my father, I was left to live with him for a couple years
while she got on her feet, and that spiraled me into feeling
never good enough, no matter what I did.

I excelled in school, always made the all-star teams
in softball and basketball, and did my chores, but it was
never good enough. He would always find something
wrong, or someone better. He would always give his good-
job pat on the backs to someone else. The pursuit of his
acknowledgement and approval really did a number on my
self-esteem, as did the abuse mentally and physically,
which I lived with for years.

I carried this "need" for approval with me into my adult years. On the exterior, this behavior displayed itself as drive, but internally, this was tearing me apart because I never felt good enough. In the military, externally this behavior showed up as me being the best soldier command had. My uniform always had the heaviest starch, the sharpest creases and my combat boots always the deepest shine possible. I would always do more push-ups, burpees and sit-ups and have one of the fastest qualifying times than the other soldiers in my units. When we were timed during events like weapons cleaning, I would always come in first, and if I did come in second or third, I would beat myself up internally. This showed up in every part of this environment, during the firing range, pursuit of medals, everything. I continually went after perfection, and when I didn't reach it, I would beat myself up and do the job internally that my father did externally. Three years into the Army and I was nominated by our company command to test for solider of the month, which on top of our regular duties and responsibilities was a significant increase in time for preparation. On testing day, I went before the board and I won. I remember my sergeant being so excited, our lieutenant sought me out to congratulate me and I was called into the first sergeant's and company commander's offices to congratulate me and let me know what was next. First off, I had never received that kind of acknowledgement, let alone attention, and I didn't know what to do with it all. Second, no one told me there was a next anything. I was sitting in their offices being given kudos that I didn't know how to handle or what to do with, so I just sat there and smiled and truly wasn't receiving, embracing and accepting them with appreciation and gratitude. They were telling me that since I'd won soldier of the month, I was in the running for soldier of the quarter, which was an even more arduous testing process with a more scrutinizing board and I would have to go up again the soldiers who had won soldier of the month within that quarter, and by winning that, I would be put in the running for soldier of the year, where the 4 winners of soldier of the quarters competed against each other to win soldier of the year. I was 21 years old and competing against 30-, 40- and 50-year-olds. I remember sitting there thinking, do they not know what I did to win this? Our regular soldier responsibilities consisted of PT (physical training) from 5am-7am, shower, eat, do our regular job, whatever that is each day from 8 am – 5 pm, then some sort of duty post multiple times a month for extended periods of times, sometimes a couple hours and sometimes we had to pull a 24-hour shift. In my "spare time," I studied for soldier of the month. And now, command was congratulating me and setting their expectation that I had to bring back a win because they had never had one. The pressure was high, and I knew I could do it. I mean seriously, sleep is overrated, right? Well, I won soldier of the quarter and soldier of the year, yet I wasn't enough. I was "only" a corporal, or I was only this or only that. I was constantly looking for things to prove I wasn't good enough.

This behavior continued in my professional career. I would climb the ranks quickly, I would make a great living financially, and I would make the company I worked for a lot of money. It didn't matter what my title was, how much money I made, because the "itty-bitty shitty committee" in my head always made me believe it wasn't good enough, I wasn't enough. The pursuit of perfection was exhausting let alone unrealistic. The concept of perfection and never doing and being enough was a hamster wheel I couldn't get off.

Corporate America introduced me to the concept and philosophy of personal and professional development. The pursuit of continually improving myself led me to learnings I never knew existed. I started studying NLP (neuro linguistics programming) and through this study, I learned that we as humans are imprinted between the ages of 0 and 7 years old, then we move to our modeling phase from 7 to 13 years old, then our socialization phase from 13 to 21 years old, and our last developmental phase is our business persona phase, which is from 21 to 29 years of age. This all helped me understand the unconscious program I was running in the background unknowingly, that I was never good enough, I had to excel in order to get attention, tear myself down and apart no matter what. None of these behaviors served me internally yet externally, I was a manager's dream from a performance perspective as long as they didn't look at that little thing called self-worth or self-esteem. I really didn't know what to do with this information, but it did help in reprogramming me.

I became a performance machine. I understood there was no such thing as perfection; it was a ruse and didn't exist. I also understood that pursuing a state of excellence did exist and was different. This new understanding and belief really showed itself when I entered the entrepreneurial environment. No matter what I embarked on, no matter what I did, I always excelled. Growth, success and money came effortlessly. People continually approached me and asked me how I kept achieving success, how everything I touched turned to gold. There were definitely some significant obstacles throughout the journey, and no matter what they were, they were always easily navigated. After a partnership split, I had been asked so many times from other entrepreneurs and salespeople for help that my purpose became clear: to make the impact I had always wanted and could never define. It had been right in front of me this whole time. I get to help people. I get to help people see and understand that it's the unknown unknowns that create the pain points in our lives and prevent us from having the life we have always dreamed of, desired and felt we had deserved. Our brains are the operating system that runs our lives. We spend so much time updating the hardware and software on our computers and our phones and all the other technologies in our lives, but we ignore the mainframe that runs everything: our brain. It's the imprints that we unknowingly carry that impact our relationships with money, health, career, beliefs, family, love, spirituality and what is and isn't important to us. That's when I created my company, Pivot Point Advantage. Now I get to serve people every day, helping them make the greatest impact in their lives and in their businesses. I realized long ago creating success has always been easy for me, and now I get to help others do the same. I feel so blessed that I get to live my purpose every second of every day. I learned that my past didn't define me. My past created me, and some of the gifts that came disguised as my greatest burdens actually became my greatest assets.

Success truly is easy. The reason why so many don't achieve their dreams is they set the bar too low and they either hit it or just miss. Stop striving to just get by. Stop allowing the itty-bitty shitty committee in your head to steal your dreams. Shoot for excellence and success will come easy. I look forward to hearing about all your successes that come your way. Allow yourself to make the impact you have always wanted. Now go make shift happen!

Stacey O'Byrne is one of the nation's leading experts in entrepreneurial transformation, evolution and success. Stacey is an international InspirActional™ speaker who specializes in Successology™, the science of success. Stacey has authored several best-selling books, with a few more being released soon. She has co-authored book with Jack Canfield and another with Jay Abrahams.

Stacey is a trainer, best-selling author, certified NLP Master Trainer, TEAM Referral Network multiple territories franchise owner and a US Army Veteran. Stacey has built two 7 figure businesses and three 6 figure businesses 100% from networking. Stacey has worked with thousands of entrepreneurs, helping them create the success they desire and deserve.

Stacey helps entrepreneurs, sales people and business owners make shift happen in their lives, businesses and bank accounts. If you mean business about business, Stacey can help you make your dreams your reality.
Stacey's' passion is working with amazing entrepreneurs

Be the Impact the World Needs

Making an impact means so many different things to so many different people. As you have read from all our expert authors, each of them has made a difference in their own lives and in the lives of others without sometimes even realizing or setting out to do so. You've heard that if a butterfly flaps its wings, it can and will create a vibrational impact across the other side of the world. No matter who you are, no matter what you do and no matter how big or small you feel your part is in this world, we can promise you, you have in the past, are currently and will in the future create some kind of impact in your life and in so many others' lives. The question you get to ask yourself is, "Is this an intentional impact?"

Our hope is this book has made an impact on you and maybe even on your life. Our desire is that these stories that our impact-driven experts have shared inspire and motivate you to allow yourself to look at things a little differently. Allow you to look at yourself, your life your dreams a little differently. Maybe you have been able to look at past experiences a little differently now and to gather valuable lessons on past experiences to create the opportunity of even more potential and possibilities.

Our wish is that you realize your true value and potential, embrace who you are and allow yourself to step into your greatness and make the impact you are here to create. We are excited to hear your stories of how our impact-driven experts have inspired you to realize the greatness you have always had and the impacts you have made in the past and the intentional impacts that you are set to create in the near and distant future.

Please feel free to reach out to us at any time at admin@pivotpointadvantage.com and share your journey with us, as well as any messages you would like us to share with our authors. We look forward to getting to know you and to seeing the impact that you get to live. Now, go make shift happen

Blessings,
Stacey and MaryLou

Made in the USA
Monee, IL
30 September 2020